# OPENING EYES
# AND EARS

# OPENING EYES AND EARS

## Kathy Lowe

## NEW CONNECTIONS FOR CHRISTIAN COMMUNICATION

With a commentary by Martin E. Marty

**World Council of Churches, Geneva
in association with
the Lutheran World Federation, Geneva,
and the World Association
for Christian Communication, London**

**For René and the cane cutters.** This book reflects the ideas, information and comments of a large number of people who believed in this project and gave of their time so generously. Warmest thanks to them, and especially to Theresa Carino, Rosie Dalziel, John Downing, Philip Hearse, Martina Krause and Porfirio Martinez Laboy.

**Cover and illustrations: Oliver Duke**
ISBN No. 2-8254-0750-X

# Contents

# Introduction

This book is a response to a crisis that has been quietly growing within the churches we serve. The crisis concerns communication credibility. Not simply because of the traditional reluctance of churches to take communication seriously (in terms of money, study, staff). The crisis is a much wider one, as the current Unesco debate on a New World Information and Communication Order makes clear, for even when churches do invest in the latest technology and the highest professionalism, there is still a disconcerting failure to open eyes and ears by gospel standards.

So something much more is at stake than any question of *how* we might communicate. There is a prior question of *what* we have to share as churches and the criteria we use to select and shape that contribution. The agencies that produced this book chose these criteria carefully. In selecting stories we looked (without attempting to balance geographical location, confession or type of media) for evidence of that which makes communication credible. That credibility was found to be best measured by such qualities as commitment to justice, cultural authenticity, participatory style, respect for spiritual mystery, openness to dialogue, clarity of purpose, appropriateness of media and style. Where these qualities are evident, within, alongside and outside the churches, there eyes and ears are opened and the gospel (when it is appropriate to talk about the gospel) is understood and shared.

The stories that illustrate this happening are modest enough. Most of them share a fragile present and an uncertain future. But all of them point to communication possibilities that together might promise some way out of the crisis.

We are grateful to Kathy Lowe for her skill and care in assembling these chapters and respecting the very different self-understandings involved, for only half the stories describe explicitly Christian contexts. Yet Martin Marty's reflection helps us see the risks and possibilities of connecting all the experiences shared here to the churches' communication task. For it is that task and its more credible pursuit that this book hopes to serve.

JOHN BLUCK
Director, WCC Department of Communication

MARC CHAMBRON
Director, LWF Department of Communication

HANS FLORIN
General Secretary, WACC

# Setting the stage
# for social change

A famous actress and a film director were among its founders. A leading journalist and an industrialist sit on its board of trustees. All the prestigious papers praise its productions. Yet until recently the Philippine Educational Theatre Association (PETA) camped rent-free in a Manila office block with four desks and a filing cabinet. Its full-time staff have been known not to receive their pay on time. Its volunteer actors, after a performance, can't always afford the fare home.

PETA's approach to drama leaves no room for prima donnas. While Manila's high society is entertained by lavish Broadway-style productions, PETA's repertory company performs at discount prices to students and workers at Fort Santiago, an intimate outdoor theatre cradled in the ruins of the old city.

*Peti-Burgis* (Petty Bourgeois) is typical of their plays, written in the Filipino language by a Filipino and performed with the simplest costumes and props. It centres on the dilemma of a petty bourgeois activist in the early 70s who becomes the personnel manager of a big company to please his father and finds himself caught up in the uncomfortable contradictions between labour and management.

Far from Manila, PETA actors can be seen in still less conventional settings. An evening may find them with a group of farmers who are improvizing costumes and acting out the problems of their village. From an assortment of mosquito nets, banana leaves, papers and old clothes characters are created and the story of a community, its people, its sufferings and its power structure, begins to unfold.

Since PETA started in 1967, the group has moved from simply trying to create a people's theatre movement to seeing the power of drama as an educational tool and finally as a weapon for communities seeking to analyze and challenge the injustice around them. Many artists have been silenced or coopted by the regime of President Ferdinand Marcos. But PETA has maintained a respected public profile and, under its protection, reached out with a team of committed actor-teachers to all sorts of groups in the slums and the poor rural areas.

In the Philippines, demands for change in the neo-colonial structure of society have always gone hand in hand with the search for a genuine Filipino culture. And popular discontent with a culture and education system shaped by centuries of Spanish and American domination grew sharper during the wave of radicalism which swept the country in the late 60s and early 70s.

Expressing opposition on any front, however, became much more dangerous with the 1972 martial law clampdown. All democratic organizations were banned, the media were muzzled, and critics of the regime imprisoned and tortured in their thousands. Nine years later martial law was lifted to clear the ground for the Pope's visit. Nevertheless, in the "New Republic" of today little has really changed. The country still has one of the lowest per capita incomes in the world, gaping social inequalities, a high inflation rate and a foreign debt which accounts for a third of the gross national product. The broad-based resistance movement composed of guerrilla organizations, trade unions, peasants associations and community groups aided by priests and nuns is still a thorn in the government's side.

National newspapers, TV and radio continue to be heavily censored. Vast sums of money are poured into propaganda films and publications portraying the regime's leaders as respected guardians of the Filipino people.

Theatre, because it is not a "mass" medium, has never been regarded by the authorities as a potential threat to the same extent as other forms of communication. During martial law (when critical ideas were often put across through historical themes) and since then, drama has remained one of the few outlets for social comment.

PETA did not begin its life as a by-product of political unrest. It was the project of famous Filipina actress-director Cecile Guidote. Guidote rejected the brand of nationalism and nationalist culture espoused by the regime. She turned down the offer of running the First Lady's Cultural Centre of the Philippines. Her own dream, and the dream of the young artists and media workers she drew around her, was to build an indigenous theatre movement which would give voice to the problems, needs and aspirations of the mass of the people.

The group's first step as PETA was to set up a training branch and a repertory company. The training branch launched courses in drama, movement, visual arts and group dynamics for students, teachers and office workers. And it was soon running workshops in the cities and provinces designed to encourage schools and colleges to create their own theatre groups. PETA's repertory branch, the Kalinangan Ensemble, put the newly trained actors from the courses to work on productions by Filipino playwrights presented at Manila's Fort Santiago.

Theatre in the cities of the Philippines has long consisted mainly of European classics performed in English for the well-to-do. Even folklore plays presented during festivals in the countryside are Spanish-influenced — large-scale productions with themes completely unrelated to people's real lives. It was this traditon of hybrid drama, plus the English plays and operettas taught in schools, that PETA set out to counter.

It wasn't easy to win the interest of students and ordinary working people and to help them to appreciate plays in their own language. For that reason Cecile Guidote and well-known film director Lino Brocka (PETA's executive director) called on big-name actors and actresses to head their casts. These performers pulled in the crowds at Fort Santiago until PETA became accepted in its own right.

Among PETA's first students were Gardy Labad, 30, who became head of training for a time, and 32 year-old Cecilia Garrucho, now advisor to the Kalinangan Ensemble.

Gardy left his seminary after six years as its organist and musical director to concentrate on composing. His strongest memory of that early period was "our concern to strive for a legitimate Filipino culture". Cecilia earns her living as host on an educational TV show. Like most members of the PETA team she gives her services to the group voluntarily. She says of Cecile Guidote: "She wanted to train artists who could really subjugate their egos — who were willing to harness their talents so they could be of use."

PETA's first link with grassroots groups, as distinct from schools, colleges and interested individuals, was forged in 1969 through the organization's administrative officer, Remmy Rikken. Remmy, a community worker, used to be based on the southern island of Mindanao with a church-backed social action centre and various farmers' organizations. She noticed that whenever there were demonstrations and meetings, the farmers tended to "dramatize" their situation.

So Remmy invited Cecile Guidote, Lino Brocka and another artist to the diocese of Tagum in Davao del Sur to conduct their first workshop with a peasant group. The experience showed how drama could be used to help people with little or no formal education to gain confidence and express themselves. It was to give PETA's work an important extra dimension in the future, paving the way for eventual workshops with community health groups in Isabella, sugar cane workers in Negros, fishermen in Binangonan, cottage industry workers in Legaspi, seminarians in Batangas and with many parish youth groups.

From early on, church organizations have been ready partners of PETA. Priests, nuns and Christian community workers struggling to support embryo labour unions and cooperatives amongst desperately poor farmers and plantation workers were keen to learn how to use drama. They saw an obvious place for it, too, in relating the gospel to people's everyday lives.

Some parishes have employed theatre techniques in creating their own liturgy. One community of sugar workers gave their annual *cenaculo* (passion play) a strong political message by using a rough cross of sugar cane — much to the indignation of plantation owners.

With martial law, PETA's budding contact with groups of this kind were suddenly rendered much more difficult. Cecile Guidote herself, feeling unable to operate under martial law conditions, went into self-imposed exile in New York, leaving the organization in something of a vacuum.

Gardy Labad and Cecilia Garrucho realized that they now had to develop a more collective style of working. And every new visit to the rural areas convinced them and others in their team that PETA's best contribution lay in linking together acting, teaching and grassroots organizing.

Gradually they stopped seeing the world through what Gardy called their "middle-class glasses". They discovered young boys suffering from hernias because of carrying too much sugar cane. They met banana plantation workers afflicted with skin diseases because they had to wash fruit sprayed with insecticide. They saw logging industry workers facing eviction because the land was needed for huge development schemes.

One trip in particular persuaded Cecilia Garrucho how worthwhile it would be to try to bring theatre within reach of more people. "I remember walking through the rice fields at night. There were some people sitting around and chatting with their neighbours. This seemed to be the only form of entertainment they had: there were no newspapers, no form of media at all. Only once a year, during the village *fiesta,* are people treated to a 'drama' which they still talk about six months later."

From 1978-80, a team of twenty PETA teachers held thirty workshops in different parts of the country, often at the invitation of parish priests. Sometimes they would have to go slowly because the people were so weary after their day's work in the fields. Or they would have to throw their syllabus out of the window and start again when they realized that the participants were illiterate. "At first people were suspicious of us," said one; "they couldn't understand why city people like us would want to spend time with them."

Gradually, a mutual trust would develop. Over games, music, improvizations and laughter, the people would begin to open up, to realize their own creative potential. Says Cecilia: "It's a miracle every time, a boost to their self-esteem and self-image. And the story they tell is always so powerful because it comes from their lives."

Visiting Japanese dramatist Masahiko Hotta sat in one PETA workshop arranged by the churches in Bacolod, a town in one of the southern islands where most of the people work on sugar plantations. He watched as the thirty participants aged between 14 and 45 were first asked to express basic emotions — anger, joy, sadness. Next they were asked to improvize costumes worn in the village, using locally available materials. Then they mimed the person in the village they most loved or hated, adding speech at the final stage.

Says Hotta: "At a certain moment one tenant imitated the middleman in the village who had always oppressed him. A girl started imitating her mother who suffered ill-treatment by this same man. Suddenly, the class transformed into a village of sugar cane workers. Characters in the village took shape — soldiers, landlords, plantation owners, workers, teacher, priest, middleman, and the various relationships between them were acted out. Eventually, in the play that emerged, the sugar plantation workers voted against the plantation owners. There was a dialogue between them that does not exist in reality."

The play ended abruptly, however, when those acting as soldiers burst in on the scene and confronted the people. "Some girls in the workshop wept," Hotta remembers. "The whole drama had come too close to their real experiences."

By the end of the 70s this new use of theatre had begun to find fertile ground in many different places at once. At PETA's suggestion, Masahiko Hotta had also visited Mindanao and discovered a Christian drama group performing a play in a Muslim fishing village. The play, presented in a church, told of a fishing village which was forced to evacuate by a US company. The priest, seminarians and coconut plantation workers in the theatre group had themselves put the play together from research and interviews made by the priest a few years earlier. They decided to bring it to the Muslim community because this community's own village was under the same threat.

Unlike these performers, PETA's actor-teachers do not usually come from the rural areas where they run a number of workshops. While they are there, though, for several days at a time, they live among the local people and find that they learn as much as they teach.

Volunteer Carme Sanchez, a college graduate and part-time film actress, says she was "a real bum" who didn't know what to do with her life. After three years of travelling around organizing PETA workshops she believes she has become a more committed person, with a much broader view of the "social realities" in her country.

Contact with activists in the field during the late 70s, including many of those influenced by liberation theology, began to push PETA away from its emphasis on drama *forms* towards grasping the nettle of the *content*. The issue crystallized in Butuan, in Mindanao, where PETA was invited to conduct a workshop with very politicized community workers and also met a number of villagers. The PETA teachers criticized the community organizers for the way they fed "structural analysis" to the people. In turn the community workers criticized PETA for their lack of social orientation and clear political direction.

It was a hard but fruitful exchange. Said the PETA people afterwards: "We are confronted with nagging questions of what use these so-called artistic and technical tools are if they could not be used in alleviating if not solving the more pressing problems that hamper an individual's or a community's growth and development."

This encounter influenced PETA's whole orientation and method of work. From then on, the team decided, the organization's curriculum would try to sharpen people's awareness of their social, political and economic environment as well as their cultural one. At the same time it would aim to develop each participant's openness, trust and sensitivity to working as part of a group.

In the countryside PETA redoubled its efforts to link up with ongoing action programmes and to talk through with villagers the problems they raised in their plays so that each group could begin to pinpoint the underlying causes of these problems and ways of tackling them.

In Manila, meanwhile, stories brought back from the rural areas and increasing contact between the PETA repertory company and leaders of the slum communities in the city had given the Kalinangan Ensemble's plays an even sharper cutting edge.

The 1979 Christmas production showed Mary and Joseph's search for an inn in a contemporary Philippines setting. The couple met oppressed fellow workers, farmers and fishermen on the one hand and the indifferent upper classes on the other. Another play told the true story of a street boy in the slums who ate lizards and mice in order to survive. The Filipina author based her material on interviews with the boy and with local people in his district. By the time the play reached the stage a slum dweller was in the cast, another had written the music and there were not enough seats in the theatre to accommodate all their neighbours trying to get in.

Exposure trips to poor areas have now become a built-in part of PETA's summer courses in Manila. When Nanette Lorico, a student at the Philippine Christian University, joined a PETA workshop in 1980 she and the other participants were sent to the slums to talk to factory workers, prostitutes and families who were being evicted from their homes.

The experience left a big impression on Nanette and she liked PETA's refusal to stress professionalism or "art for art's sake". Under her leadership, the university repertory club is now performing its own plays among slum dwellers and factory workers.

The church-backed Asian Social Institute in Manila conducted an evaluation of PETA's workshops in 1982, interviewing a sample of 76 people from 25 groups in 15 provinces. The researchers concluded: "There is still need for PETA to reach out to more deserving communities." However, from those communities already reached they gained extremely positive feedback. None of the local theatre groups they visited viewed drama merely as a form of entertainment but as a way of raising people's consciousness. They had written and directed their own productions, used original scripts depicting local situations and had involved the audience in reflecting on the message of the play.

PETA's approach to theatre is producing a definite ripple effect outside the country as well. Masahiko Hotta from Tokyo's Black Tent Theatre was one of the first foreigners to take part in PETA summer workshops in 1978. His evaluation of the workshops helped to push through the idea of an exchange between PETA and other Asian artists. And two years later PETA had a new offshoot, the Asian Theatre Forum (ATF), with Hotta as its coordinator.

To find an Asian identity through the use of theatre which is "for the people and by the people" is ATF's aim. Each summer an ATF workshop brings together some thirty artists and social workers from Papua New Guinea, Thailand, Malaysia, Singapore, Japan and the Philippines. For six intensive weeks they live and work under the same roof, sleeping 13 to a room in spartan conditions in converted classrooms. They learn about theatre for concientization. They compare theatre techniques and traditions from their countries and discuss the social, economic and political situation there. Says Cecilia Garrucho: "We all share a common political profile. Repression is everywhere. Wealth is in the hands of the very few. Transnational corporations have invaded Asian countries. In this context (we) have much to share and learn from each other."

Participants are trained to train others on their return home and PETA staff have followed up with extra assistance on the spot in the case of Papua New Guinea, Singapore, Malaysia and Indonesia. "Our dream", says Cecilia Garrucho, "is to have a core of South East Asian teachers who are committed to bring theatre within reach of the people."

The dream may not be far off. Two Indian participants, following their 1980 visit to Manila, have initiated a whole chain of grassroots drama groups. And Japan's Black Tent Theatre movement, which used to lay great stress on professionalism and to see theatre as a one-way process, has adopted PETA's people-oriented techniques. Says Masahiko Hotta: "Now I'm more of an educator than a dramatist. It was PETA that changed me."

PETA continues to grow, and yet somehow manages to avoid becoming top heavy. Amazingly there is a secretariat of only five full-time staff. The bulk of the work is taken care of by a core of about eighty active members. They divide themselves into teams —

for writing, directing, movement, fund-raising etc. Each team elects a representative to sit on the executive committee and these team leaders plus board members take the overall policy and money decisions.

Actress-teacher Carme Sanchez and PETA's full-time accountant, Josefina Olado, say staff and members feel very involved in decision-making and that women, who make up about half the total number of volunteers, take anything but a backseat role.

A chronic lack of funds means that teamwork and the commitment of volunteers count for everything. Chairman Teodoro Valencia argues that the shortage of money has forced PETA to be more resourceful and creative over the years. Nevertheless, the organization is showing the strain of operating for so long on a shoe-string budget.

Because PETA can't afford to pay its actor-teachers they are forced to take on other jobs for their economic survival which detracts from the time and energy they can put into PETA activities. What little money the Kalinangan Ensemble makes goes into maintaining the secretariat so there is hardly anything left over to plough back into equipment.

Until recently the only external funding was a grant from a German church agency for the Asia exchange programme, the rest coming from donations and the Kalinangan Ensemble. Plans are afoot to approach business people to donate to a trust fund, and a new $100,000 grant from a Dutch agency should soon take off the immediate pressure but the longer-term problem remains.

Another weakness is a lack of systematic follow-up of workshop groups and the fact that PETA, for all its dedication, is not rooted as an organization in the communities it helps, nor directly sharing in their actions for change.

Certainly, PETA has a wide mix of members and backers, including influential names, and their goal of a people's theatre movement binds them together. But not all, as Remmy Rikken acknowledges, have the same deep social and political commitment or the same inclination to engage in grassroots work. In the Philippines context, with a political threat always in the shadows, there may come a time when strong internal unity and a broad base of support among workers and peasants could prove the deciding factors.

Will PETA be able to anticipate future obstacles and deal with them in good time? That remains to be seen. But having come through so much and having achieved so wide an impact with so few material resources, members are quick to spot possible pitfalls.

Meanwhile, what was only a hope for them 15 years ago is rapidly turning into reality as more and more local drama groups spring up around the countryside and dramatists like Masahiko Hotta take home a concept of theatre "not only as art, but also a great weapon for the masses".

# Claiming a space to speak out

It was 7.45 in the morning when the telephone rang in the editor's home. "The paper's out," announced the delighted voice of his colleague Christel Schiller. What for most newspapers would have been an everyday announcement was a relief for the staff of *Mecklenburgische Kirchenzeitung,* a Lutheran weekly paper in the German Democratic Republic.

This issue of the paper had touched on a proposal by some young Christian peace campaigners in the German Democratic Republic that conscientious objectors should be allowed to choose community work ("social peace service") as an alternative to military service. Differences over this between church and state were still being thrashed out. So the staff of *MKZ* had despatched their paper to the printers not knowing whether it would appear or lead to talks with the state press office. Only when Christel Schiller spotted her postman carrying copies in his satchel did she know for sure that it was being distributed.

These kinds of tensions are nothing out of the ordinary for the *MKZ* team, given that their paper differs in no small measure from both the state-dominated press of the GDR and its church counterparts in other regions of the country. Says editor Gerhard Thomas:

"Our room for manoeuvre as church press is bigger than many people think and we must use it. We can do a lot."

*MKZ* is one of five Protestant and two Catholic papers in the GDR, a country hailed as the economic success story of Eastern Europe and one of the top ten industrial powers in the world. As for the secular press, each of the four political parties runs its own national and regional daily papers. These have extremely limited independence from a state in which the Communist Party holds the monopoly of power.

The headquarters of the Evangelical Lutheran Church of Mecklenburg, in the small lakeside town of Schwerin, houses *MKZ*'s unpretentious single-storey office. The paper's circulation area covers the once agricultural, now fast industrializing, northern zone of Mecklenburg, bounded in the north by the Baltic sea and by Poland in the east.

*MKZ* has to operate in a setting where the church in Luther's homeland, after centuries of enjoying national status and having its church taxes collected on its behalf by the government, now finds itself a minority group separated off in a secular society.

How it sees that society was summed up recently by the President of the Federation of Protestant Churches, Dr Albrecht Schönherr. He told a World Council of Churches Central Committee meeting in Dresden: "As members of the ecumenical community, GDR Christians are strengthened in their resolve neither to conform uncritically to (this) socialist society... nor to reject it in principle." Recalling the days of Naziism which he said had tried to turn the church into a pliable tool, Dr Schönherr added that "the German churches are sensitive to ideological distortion".

From the church's point of view, a big improvement in its relations with the state came in 1978 when, after an arduous discussion process, GDR leader Erich Honecker and the Church Federation agreed the principle of the church as an autonomous institution and partner within socialism. From the state's point of view, while it values the contribution of the churches through, for example, the diaconal homes and hospitals they maintain, it feels that Christians have yet to show themselves to be wholehearted partners.

GDR Christians today (of all confessions) are thought to number somewhere between 7 and 8.5 million out of a 17 million population. The situation of churches whose congregations have dwindled, whose financial resources are scarce and whose task is to witness in very changed circumstances, is one in which a uniting, outward-looking church press can play a crucial role.

At first glance, *MKZ* seems a bit staid. It carries the usual parish news and announcements, has cumbersome-sized pages, old-fashioned type-styles and a name which means, simply, "Church Paper of Mecklenburg". Yet, in the words of one Berlin-born specialist in East European affairs, it is an effort "to make the church an alternative to the uniformity in the whole country".

Among other things the paper has critically reported politically sensitive issues such as nuclear energy, ecology, Poland, nuclear disarmament and the unjust distribution of wealth and power between the richest and poorest countries. But it is *MKZ*'s concept of a paper as the "property" of its readers, and the way it puts this philosophy into practice, that makes it unusual in any context.

Columns "give a voice" to those who are frequently denied a fair hearing in church and society — women, youth and children — and they help to prepare material themselves. Church readers' groups around the country of workers, students and families discuss the articles and feed in their criticisms, ideas and information needs.

A network of correspondents, pastors and lay people all over the region send in news, meditations, reviews, etc. Through regular meetings with the staff, they make a substantial input as a group into shaping the content of the paper.

Gerhard Thomas, wiry, chain-smoking, always on the move, is a self-taught journalist and was once a volunteer correspondent during his time as a local pastor. His colleague, Christel Schiller, who has worked on the paper for many years, still teases him about his early creative efforts. "I remember that meditation about Mary and Joseph on the motorbike," she smiles.

Today Gerhard is a widely respected writer in the ecumenical movement, a member of the Lutheran World Federation's communications commission and one of the main movers behind efforts to launch a new press service for European Lutheran minority churches.

Producing *MKZ*, he explains, presents many practical as well as ideological constraints. All GDR newspapers are licenced by the state and distributed by mail to subscribers. *MKZ*'s popularity convinces staff that they could push up the circulation and put the paper on a more viable footing. However, under the licence a ceiling has been imposed on the amount of newsprint they can buy so they cannot go any higher than four pages or sell more than the current 15,000 copies. Nor can they increase the subscription price which is frozen at 0.18 marks* per copy.

---

* One US dollar = DM 2.35.

Another blow came in 1977 when the publishing house of the ruling Socialist Unity Party (SED), which prints the paper, raised its rates by 30% because of changing to a more expensive printing process. The net result is that the Lutheran Church of Mecklenburg has to pump in a hefty subsidy of 20,000 marks a year to keep its weekly paper going.

The synod will keep to its commitment, says Oberkirchenrat Siegert, the church's head of finance and administration, because it believes in *MKZ*'s "strong spiritual mission". The editor's problems were the church's problems although "it is sometimes difficult to explain to congregations why the paper is not making propaganda for leading church bodies".

All those involved in *MKZ* have worked hard to convince their constituency that their paper can never be a simple mouthpiece. The location of their office, across the courtyard from the main Lutheran complex, symbolizes their relationship to the church institution — "independent, not separate".

In this office, one rainy morning in November, the regular weekly editorial meeting is in progress. Pressed around the page plans are Gerhard Thomas, his deputy editor, 30 year old Jurgen Kapiske, formerly a pastor-correspondent in the Berlin-Brandenburg region, administrator Christel Schiller, and trainee production assistant Regina Dietrich, aged 20.

Christel left her first job with *MKZ* to join a secular paper in Mecklenburg but came back because, she says, "I preferred to be where I could express my own opinions". Regina changed her mind about studying to become a history teacher. "I like the plurality of the work on the paper." The two women plus part-time secretary Hella Beutler are paid out of the newspaper's budget in line with church rates for its office workers. The two men receive slightly higher pastor's salaries.

Everyone chips in suggestions for the next week's paper plan. The atmosphere is relaxed, the teamwork obvious. "The synod report will need more space..." "That pic on page four won't work very well..." "Let's bring forward the letter from the women..."

That same afternoon Regina, Jurgen and Gerhard drive up in front of a neat detached house in nearby Kühlungsborn. Waiting for them are three local women who want to talk about how to develop the coverage of women's concerns in the paper. One is a pastor, the second a lay leader in a local congregation and a member of the church council. The third is a photographer with no church connection whose pictures have been published in *MKZ*.

The three women had already sent a letter to the paper pointing out the low representation of women on church bodies. They appealed to other women to help them form a group and use *MKZ* to raise some problems of discrimination which affected them all.

Now the discussion revolves around how to follow up that first initiative. Thoughts on subjects to tackle in the future are tossed around while the two men take a back seat. "The law says we have equal rights but many aspects of daily life mitigate against this..." "Women do a double job because they have families to look after too..." "Housework isn't recognized as real work. I don't know of one family where the woman and man share the tasks equally..." "My mother looks after my sick grandmother as well as doing the housework. And she loses her self-esteem because she can't be financially independent..."

Future themes tackled, they decide, should include problems of single mothers, financial independence, the implications for child development when mothers go out to work. "Women in those situations should write the articles," Gerhard Thomas proposes.

The following day Gerhard, who spends a large slice of time driving at breakneck speed along Mecklenburg's country roads, drops in on two pastor "co-workers" in Neubrandenburg. The town is typical of many others in the region, a fast-expanding urban centre with people pouring in from other areas to swell the work force of the factories.

Pastors Martin Seidel and Fritz Rabe see the situation of the church in Neubrandenburg as typical too. Some 5,000 people out of a population of 32,000 are registered church members and local congregations draw in about 800. "That's why", say the pastors, "not only the experiences of practising Christians must be fed into *MKZ,* but also those of the many whose connections with the church are more tenuous."

They have both produced articles drawn from their parish experience debating how to witness as Christians participating in a socialist society. This material hadn't gone down too well with some church leaders who said that witnessing, not participating in socialism, was their concern. A number of lay people, on the other hand, had been keen to follow up the articles in church discussion groups.

A Bible study written by Martin Seidel for one issue of *MKZ* led to talks with the state press department and was withdrawn by staff before the paper's publication. The item in question was a colloquial, modernized account of Jeremiah's tribulations as a critical voice in his society.

Gerhard Thomas's next port of call is a church readers' group in the little country town of Wesenberg. The group is meeting over glasses of wine in Harald and Illeane Weinrebe's pastor house. Harald is church superintendent for the surrounding district. Illeane takes charge of religious education for the children of the Wesenberg congregation. Others present include the local baker, kindergarten teacher and builder, plus choirmaster and several older church members who are retired.

"We value your feedback because without it we would be very isolated," Gerhard tells them, asking for reactions to recent issues of the paper. Everyone seems to have something to say. More international stories was one request. "We don't have much chance of getting such information and we need this contact."

The children's corner, written by and about children from different parishes, was thought to be fun — and useful because it enabled parents to show their children that, as Christians, they weren't alone. "They tend to feel the odd ones out at school."

The question of style came up. "Wasn't last week's back page story a bit highbrow?" suggests someone. "Perhaps," says her neighbour, "but generally the paper writes like people speak."

The letters page was regarded as an effective way of keeping a dialogue going. "It's important to show differences of opinion within the church. It's a sign that the church is alive."

The group agreed that the secular papers, as compared with *MKZ*, gave the impression that their society had no problems. "Our paper, on the other hand, helps us make up our own minds."

Gerhard confides that the staff of the paper had consciously decided, in the current issue of *MKZ*, to mention the Christian youth suggestion of community work as an alternative to military service. They knew that the whole question of peace campaigning and the youth's demand for unilateral disarmament was hotly disputed. (The state regards Soviet missiles as necessary to keep peace and says that conscientious objectors already have the option of performing military service in non-combat units). But it was important, Gerhard declared, "to go on trying to give correct reports like this with no unnecessary self-censorship".

Back in Schwerin, Gerhard returns to the censorship issue. He believes in discussing the limitations the staff work under with readers, but, he says: "I want to show people I speak to that all is not black here and white in the West." Absolute press freedom, he and

Jurgen Kapiske insist, is an illusion anywhere. They see Western journalists as operating under their own constraints, obliged, for instance, to sell their writing to media which are commercial commodities.

In such a conversation, the Federal Republic of Germany is the obvious point of comparison. "The West German press wants to give readers its version of events like the secular press in the GDR," argues Jurgen. And the press there, in Gerhard's view, was often one-sided. Some papers portrayed GDR churches as being in the pocket of the state while they themselves often sided with ruling groups, even those led by politicians known for their one-time Nazi sympathies.

In both the GDR and FRG, Gerhard believes, media workers have to try to find what free space exists and try to expand it. A church correspondent with one of Mecklenburg's secular dailies says Gerhard practises what he preaches. "He is going to the end of his limits. I sometimes feel that I'm not going to the end of mine."

Because the people of the GDR, through contact with their German relatives across the border and their possibility of picking up FRG TV programmes in most parts of the country, are susceptible to ideological influence from this direction, this is all the more reason, according to the staff of *MKZ*, to offer a GDR paper with its own independent Christian perspective.

The GDR, for example, has a number of atomic energy plants. In so far as these are mentioned in the secular press, it is primarily from the standpoint that they are essential for supplying the country's power needs. *MKZ* joins in this debate but also underlines the ecological and safety aspects.

In another instance, the secular newspapers said that talks between the US National Council of Churches and the Federation of Protestant Churches in the GDR had dealt with nuclear weapons and called for peace and disarmament in the USA. In fact, as *MKZ* reported, the meeting came out in favour of disarmament in the US *and in the Soviet Union.*

*MKZ* staff call their policy one of "critical solidarity". It is an attempt not to make general judgments on socialist society but to offer criticisms as citizens *within* it. Says Gerhard Thomas: "I'm not anticommunist and I don't want to put the clock back. Under socialism we have social care, health care, security of employment and the same chance of education for everyone." Nonetheless, he added his society was not perfect and needed development that everyone could take part in. "There's too much dogma. That's a point where the dialogue between church and state has to start."

In its own way *MKZ* is already stimulating dialogue between Christians and socialists at the local level. When readers show the paper to their work mates or fellow students they report that these friends "begin to see that the church is more than a congregation". Gerhard Thomas's son, Roger, has used his father's articles on disarmament in discussions with other young soldiers while on military service.

At a church discussion group in Rostock on the Baltic coast, the subject of *MKZ* came up and led to a more general exchange on subjects covered by the paper such as education, nuclear arms, racism and colonialism. One young woman sat silently throughout, then suddenly spoke up. She made it clear that she was not a Christian and had only accompanied her husband because she wanted to understand better his religious beliefs. She said she was surprised by the openness of the debate and felt that many Marxists shared the concerns that had surfaced. "Now I'm persuaded that there's a lot of scope for us all to discuss and work together."

One well-known Marxist journalist and intellectual recently made a brief critique of *MKZ* as a contribution to a policy meeting of staff and co-workers. He made a number of practical layout suggestions, then praised the Bible studies and theological debates as giving "a full picture of church praxis in our time". By way of a postscript he added: "As Marxists and Christians I believe we have a lot of ideals in common. Only at the cemetery will we part company, since for Marxists the grave will remain closed while for Christians it stays open for always."

Not everyone sees the situation in this light. Anti-communist feelings still run high in some church circles as demonstrated by indignant letters received when *MKZ* has criticized Western European or North American decision-makers. Also, there is a very vocal and influential body of people in the GDR church structures who see the mission of Christians in the country, and therefore the mission of the Christian press, as one of making propaganda for the church. In view of all this, as another Lutheran Church official put it: "*MKZ* can promote a dialogue but in order to do so it must be critical of the church too."

A cursory flip through any issue of the paper is enough to convince the reader that this challenge has been taken on board. The very scope of the theological, social and international coverage — all with a strongly ecumenical flavour — is clearly intended to help the church to become more confident and outward-looking. Themes of recent articles and letters include children's right to take communion, the changing roles of women and men in the church, the Bulgarian Orthodox Church, a radical missionary group in India, apartheid, common law marriage, homosexuality...

Youth, women and children are seen as vital to the change and renewal of the church. So their input in the form of stories, poems and interviews they write themselves is given a high priority, as is their participation in small editorial groups where they decide in collaboration with the journalists what subject to tackle and how.

The staff of the paper are involved in the life of the church in a variety of ways. Jurgen and Gerhard are frequent guest speakers in local parishes and run a two-day communications awareness session as part of a course for trainee pastors. Christel Schiller and Hella Beutler are both active in their home congregations.

Regina Dietrich is trying to get the local women's group under way. On the position of the women on *MKZ* she notes that despite the teamwork, since the journalists are men and those in the back-up jobs are women "you don't have such a big say if you're a woman on the staff because the final decisions lie with the writers".

For the future, Gerhard Thomas feels encouraged by the continuing backing of his church of Mecklenburg. But he is the first to admit that the paper is only as strong as the constituency it serves. For him, the network of co-workers which meets with staff several times a year to hammer out new policies and tasks is far more than just a source of feedback and extra material. It is one essential way of constructing a wide base of support among lay people, youth and pastors in the ranks of the church for the ideas the paper stands for.

Only if such a broad lobby is built will *Mecklenburgische Kirchenzeitung* be able to go on playing an effective part in the process of opening up and dialogue which is so close to its heart.

# Catalyst for community struggles

A metalworker from a dormitory suburb in Rio de Janeiro tells an interviewer what happened when he and his workmates went on strike to try to stop cuts in jobs...

An Indian leader from the Amazon swaps ideas with researchers documenting the story of his tribe — pushed off its homelands to make way for agribusiness...

Families from a Sao Paulo shantytown crowd around charts and drawings at a local church, preparing themselves to vote in the first general election many have ever experienced...

These three different experiences in different parts of Brazil have one thing in common. The interviewer, researcher and church animators involved are all linked into the Ecumenical Centre for Documentation and Information (CEDI).

It's some years since a number of Protestant pastors, lay people and students based around Rio de Janeiro and Sao Paulo first came together "as an act of self-defence". Condemned by their denominations for wanting a church in solidarity with the poor and forced to keep a low profile by the 1964 military coup, they started a small information service — CEDI's predecessor — under the hardest possible conditions.

Yet CEDI today is awareness-raising. It links oppressed groups and records their struggles. This is no small contribution in a situation where people's movements are still cutting their teeth and where Brazil's media are more inclined to report the after-dinner speeches of US President Reagan than the needs of the mass of the people.

CEDI's headquarters is a honeycomb of offices hidden away behind a college in the heart of Rio de Janeiro. Charts, files and mailing lists fill every spare corner. There are constant phone calls with the second office in Sao Paulo. Discussions with visiting pastors and community workers continue non-stop in meeting rooms, in corridors, and over coffee in the kitchen.

Some overspill offices adjacent to the main building serve as a base for CEDI's team of field-workers who represent one arm of the organization. They collaborate on request with community leaders who are assisting workers' and peasants' groups in educating and organizing themselves.

The documentation service upstairs is the second arm of CEDI. It furnishes the field-workers with information on specific issues, keeps records of campaigns and activities of struggling groups across the country, and maintains a reference library for community use. Thirdly there is the publications department, a busy thoroughfare by the main door, charged with presenting the oppressed groups' actions in a popular form. It publicizes them widely through the church network so as to help emerging people's movements to learn from each other and push forward their campaigns for change.

Such change is long overdue in Brazil. People know the country as Latin America's one-time economic miracle, land of the resource-rich Amazon and of vast cities where luxury apartments and hotels rub shoulders with some of the worst slums in the world.

Many Christians know Brazil as the place where, after dictatorship drove the Catholic church underground, a new network of grassroots ecclesial communities took shape — worshipping groups under lay leadership which try to apply the Bible's teaching in their situation of social and economic injustice.

Throughout the late 60s and 70s these communities, currently estimated at 80,000 nation-wide, provided the only alternative arena in which opposition groups could organize against state repression. Now, though, a bigger space is opening up. The Brazilian regime, its economic miracle in tatters, is trying to cultivate friends abroad by cleaning up its image, toning down overt political persecution, relaxing press censorship. It finally held elections in late 1982.

The result has been a wave of strikes and land occupations, the growth of Brazil's first independent Workers' Party (PT) started by rank-and-file trade unionists, and a mushrooming of autonomous people's organizations. Peasant groups, labour movement activists and whole neighbourhoods, after hard years of consciousness-raising and organizing underground, are openly pressing for better living and working conditions.

CEDI is only one of scores of groups backing up these efforts but it has chosen a specific point at which to do it. Explains CEDI general secretary, Zwinglio Dias: "We are at the intersection of the church and the social movements. We're struggling for a better quality of relation between the two."

Zwinglio, a Presbyterian pastor who leaves his paperwork at the end of each week to take church services in a local shantytown, is one of CEDI's early members. The original Protestant group started, he remembers, by publishing biblical reflections and a small bulletin. Then they joined forces with a number of like-minded Roman Catholics and together became "one of the strongest voices of the ecumenical movement in Brazil". They went official as CEDI in 1974. The "pastoral agents" — pastors, priests and Christian neighbourhood leaders — who used their materials then are still among their main partners today.

From being a group of 15, mainly volunteers, CEDI has expanded over recent years into an organization of seven full-time coordinators plus 35 part-time staff and 10 voluntary helpers. The fieldwork or *assessoria* side of their operation came about when people interested in the publications began to ask for assistance in developing education projects in their parishes and dioceses. And it is this long-standing interaction with grassroots groups which has obviously put flesh on CEDI's philosophy of information-at-the-service-of-people-in-struggle.

For example, CEDI became involved in Sao Paulo, where people from overcrowded shantytowns have been invading land which speculators had withheld, demanding the right to settle permanently there and to receive basic services. Following violent confrontations with police in many suburbs, some communities were trying to join together to resist eviction and fight their case with local and central government.

One such group in Monte Tao called in CEDI field-workers to help them make an audiovisual story, using photographs and tape-recorded interviews with families, of how and why they took over their land. Says Henrique Pereira Júnior, the CEDI coordinator involved: "The people are going to use this audiovisual presentation to ask for support in other parts of Sao Paulo and CEDI and others will train the local people to show it and organize discussions."

In Pilar, a poor dormitory township of Rio, badly hit by unemployment, 3,000 metalworkers from a nearby Fiat truck plant downed tools in May 1981 after the company fired 200 men. CEDI workers, already backing the grassroots ecclesial community there, found themselves well placed to help build support for those strikers and their families living in the Pilar neighbourhood.

After holding out for nearly two months to try and get their workmates reinstated, the metalworkers finally conceded defeat. The story didn't end there, though. Explained CEDI coordinator José Ricardo Ramalho: "This was the first strike in Brazil fought to guarantee jobs. Some workers still don't realize the importance of what they did so CEDI is putting together a dossier of interviews with some strikers to record what happened." Local people, he added, would not forget the police repression of these workers and the victimization their leaders suffered at the hands of the company when the dispute ended. The dossier would become part of a continuing campaign in the area against unemployment. Plans for a public day of action were already in the pipeline.

If peasants' and workers' battles are the obvious pressure points for change in Brazil today, CEDI has also been focusing on those in society whose exploitation is less well recognized — women and the Brazilian Indians.

On International Women's Day 1981, CEDI's ecumenical monthly magazine *Presença* ("Witness") collaborated with several women's organizations on a special issue. Articles examined the Bible and theology from a woman's perspective. A photo feature looked at a day in the life of a woman in a Rio slum, showing her double oppression as an unpaid worker in the home and a second-class worker outside it. A panel headed "capitalist society's myths about women" challenged common assertions such as the division of labour between the sexes being the "natural" order of things.

The plight of Brazil's Indians, driven into uninhabitable territories and left destitute because of the land grab by giant state and private enterprises, is a highly explosive issue. Up to now, the government has kept sole control of information about what is happening to the Indians nation-wide, thereby hampering efforts to defend their interests. That's why, with the help of some 600 anthropologists, missionaries and Indian leaders, CEDI decided to carry out its own national survey on the changing situation of the different tribes over the last twenty years.

It's an ambitious undertaking, with photos and maps as well as data, which are sent back for checking at local level at regular stages of the production process. The survey is designed to strengthen the knowledge and development efforts of priests and nuns working alongside the Indian communities. Above all, it aims to give the tribes and their allies an overview of the Indians' situation, so preparing the ground for a national Indian movement. Says Carlos "Beto" Ricardo who coordinates this survey work from CEDI's Sao Paulo office: "It's a movement when you put different kinds of fighters in touch with one another."

In CEDI's experience, the more the groups begin to try to link up their different concerns and actions the more they feel the need for their own sources of news told from their own perspective. The poor can't afford TV, radio, or even newspapers. "People don't know what's going on even 500 miles away," explains José Ricardo Ramalho, "and newspapers are always lying about what's happening."

This problem led to CEDI launching its own duplicated weekly news digest, *Aconteceu* ("It Happened") which José Ricardo edits. The only CEDI publication aimed directly at trade unionists, peasants and community leaders, its short news pieces consist of items culled from the main newspapers supplemented by information from partner groups around the country. Says José Ricardo: "We don't want to be neutral — we have an option for the working class. I select what will interest workers, about workers, because they're the most exploited and they're the ones who are going to change society."

This approach stands in sharp contrast to that of the Brazilian mass media. Traditionally owned by the country's wealthiest families and now, increasingly, by business conglomerates, the major newspapers and magazines are very much in the US mould. The bulk of their international coverage originates from transnational news agencies. Domestic coverage, though not directly censored as in the past, gives noticeable prominence to the government's point of view.

CEDI's documentation archives, put together with information from the Brazilian press plus local and church sources, often reflect differing versions of the same events. Documentation coordinator Letícia Cotrim gives as an example the land dispute in Ronda Alta, in the southernmost state. Here the government tried to move small farmers out to the Amazon region in order to make way for land development companies. The big newspapers focused mainly on those families who had accepted resettlement. Lutheran church newsletters, on the other hand, sent to CEDI from the region, have continued to follow the fortunes of the majority. These farmers, who had camped in protest in the main street, insisted on their legal right to remain in their state of origin, Rio Grande do Sul, and were put under guard by the army in a special camp.

Other material in CEDI's archives covers subjects like faith and politics, the women's movement, industrialization and popular education. A particular effort is made to research the origins and history of activities in these different fields. Says José Ricardo: "It's important to have (such) a record. Workers in Brazil don't have a written history."

Whereas once the research and documentation was for internal use only, CEDI's small, well organized library is now open to pastors, community animators, trade unionists and academics doing social research, among many others. Every effort is made to discuss with them and match up material available to their particular needs.

Letícia Cotrim argues that this kind of behind-the-scenes input is just as vital as the more visible grassroots support. And it has sparked off some inventive action. At a recent workshop of CEDI staff and pastoral agents one young priest, Geraldo Rodrigues, told how he and others were starting a People's Information Centre in their Sao Paulo diocese of Sao Miguel. They had already run a media awareness experiment, getting a group of youth to compare TV and press coverage of problems like unemployment with the misery of the jobless as seen in their own neighbourhood. "They realized", said Geraldo, "that the TV talked about unemployment but didn't say *why* people were out of work."

Some of the youth went on to produce their own news in the form of a church bulletin board. Another group has started the use of makeshift puppets to tell the story of local people's problems.

Research done by the documentation team and presented in a special issue of *Aconteceu* had also led to some lively local meetings on the 1982 elections. When the regime promised elections CEDI workers thought it important to help people understand the whole election process and come to a more informed choice about who they wanted to vote for, especially as many had never known anything other than a military dictatorship. Extensive interviews were conducted with political party organizers and the election candidates. The resulting material clearly explained, with illustrations, how the electoral system works, and summarized the positions of all the different parties represented.

Sociologist Heloisa Martins described how she had helped to organize a local district meeting in east Sao Paulo about parties and candidates in the elections, using simple picture sheets based on the CEDI material. "The women and young children had never discussed politics before. Now they're very excited to talk about who is who."

A young priest in the same city zone, who runs a course in basic politics in Burgo Paulista, said he found CEDI's material in general "too heavy and solid" to use directly with local groups. "But the (pastoral) agents really read it and use it," he added.

CEDI produces a lot of detailed, expensive-looking materials which demand a fairly good level of education on the part of the reader. This begs the question as to whether it isn't limiting its potential audience unnecessarily. Publications coordinator Domincan Paulo Botas defends his approach as consistent with CEDI's overall objective of working primarily through pastoral agents. The materials on theology, politics and social and economic issues were intended as a resource for pastors, priests, nuns and lay leaders to draw on and adapt as they saw fit, he explained. Also it was possible to produce attractive, highly visual publications cheaply because committed photographers and artists often gave their services almost free.

One photo supplement on the building trade featured in *Presença* magazine had been used in an evening school for young apprentices. A future publications project aims to bring together half a dozen black leaders to help devise educational material about the growing black movement in Brazil. "Publications must de-block the mind. That's the political and pedagogical purpose of my work," Paulo Botas says.

CEDI understands its mandate as strengthening the relationship between the churches and the people's movements. It therefore sees the task of education and awareness-building in the churches themselves as integral to the whole process. The theological debates, Bible studies and ecumenical news published are one contribution. So too was assistance given to Sao Paulo's Cardinal Arns recently in publishing a frank, detailed report on "Repression of the Church in Brazil 1968-78".

Operating in a strongly Catholic culture, where many priests and nuns have made a clear option for the poor, has meant that CEDI, despite its Protestant roots, has developed a working partnership primarily with Catholic activists over the years. However, the organization's 1981 assembly decided to make forging links with certain Protestant denominations a new priority.

Traditionally a ghettoized 10 per cent of the population, the Protestant groups, Pentecostals excepted, tend to be conservative off-shoots of foreign churches and are more prosperous than the Catholics. With a number of their own universities and a string of famous colleges they represent an important social force which the government could try to manipulate and set against the Catholics for its own ends. That is why CEDI staff believe it is urgent to support those Protestants who want to participate in efforts for social change. As a first stage, a CEDI fieldwork team is involved in discussion groups on worship, theology and social issues with some 50 pastors from Lutheran, Presbyterian, Methodist and Episcopal churches.

The very fact that most CEDI staff and volunteers do not fit neatly into any confessional compartment themselves ("we don't ask for a Christian identity card") makes it easier for them to work with people across the religious spectrum. At the same time it could afford them less protection from the church, should Brazil's dictators decide to try to tighten their grip once again.

The decision to work with church partners rather than go directly to the different people's organizations also produces its own contradictions. Zwinglio Dias acknowledges that "the church as an institution wants to control the popular movements". Also, some committed pastoral agents, long used to a situation where the church was the only channel for those who had no voice, tend to be over-protective of local communities in the face of up-and-coming political parties and workers' organizations. One CEDI field-worker put it plainly: "We try to talk to the agents so that they won't slow the movements down."

Without funding from church agencies outside the country, CEDI could not carry on. Ninety per cent of the 1983 of $91,612 will come from foreign donors. Staff agree that this is far from ideal but they point out that it is hard to raise funds openly inside the country and that the church in Brazil is itself poor and very dependent on money from outside sources.

The profileration of CEDI's activities is another sensitive issue at this point in its evolution. Stresses Beto Ricardo: "We have reached the limit (in size). To become a big institution would be our death."

The Indian survey is one recent area of expansion. It is to be published in 19 volumes over five years at a cost of $40,000 for research and $16,000 for salaries and publishing costs. This cost represents only 20 per cent of the total expense incurred, the bulk being covered by various collaborating bodies which have loaned people and facilities. And the valuable data being gathered is available nowhere else. Nonetheless the project is claiming a considerable share of staff time and resources. It demonstrates the added pressure, in the Brazilian situation, on organizations like CEDI to take on tasks which institutions in the public eye may be unable to tackle in the same way.

Possible dangers aside, there are many features of CEDI which look likely to keep it self-critical and healthy. Not least among these is the high level of participation by pastoral partners and the organization's own internal democracy. All field-work support and information inputs are devised and evaluated with local communities themselves. Leaders of people's movements are regular participants at staff meetings as well as particular workshops.

There are no salary differentials for employees doing the same work and all paid and voluntary staff have a vote at the policy-making assembly where they elect their coordinators and the general secretary. CEDI's commitment to people's participation had to be reflected in its own structures, Zwinglio Dias explained.

There is hardly anyone among CEDI's older staff members who hasn't experienced hardship, persecution and/or exile during Brazil's toughest years of dictatorship. They don't know whether the present "relaxation" will last, but they are determined to make the most of it and go on sowing the seeds of a very different society. Their vision comes across in a recent booklet about sugar-cane workers. Under a photo of a sugar plantation the caption reads: "One piece of sugar cane is nothing, together they make a whole field."

# Loosening the grip
# of media monopolies

To all intents and purposes Mario Osava *is* Inter Press Service Third World News Agency (IPS) in Brazil. The Brazilian journalist can be located, with difficulty, down a labyrinth of corridors several floors up, in a Rio de Janeiro office block. The building, housing an assortment of organizations in Rio's commercial quarter, has seen better days. It's a safe bet that the two rooms ankle deep in telexes used by this IPS correspondent would fit into one corner of the news rooms of the big daily papers nearby.

From here, helped only by a part-time colleague, Mario Osava files at least three stories a day about Brazil for Inter Press Service's local and international subscribers. He also translates into Portuguese and pushes to Brazilian outlets material supplied to him in Spanish from other parts of his news agency's network. Facilities that other news agency journalists normally take for granted, like unlimited telex back-up, long distance phone calls and money to travel inside the country, are for him carefully rationed-out luxuries. On the face of it he is one man covering the biggest third world country in the southern hemisphere with the minimum of material support. Yet, he insists: "We can supply the kind of analysis and features they (the major news agencies) would not produce."

Inter-Press, based in Rome, Italy, is a strange animal by the standards of the brash world of press agencies. In fact it is unique. Say its staff: "We treat news as a social right, not merely as a commercial commodity."

The agency's resources are minute compared with those of giants like United Press International (UPI), Associated Press (AP), Agence France Press (AFP), the Soviet agency Tass and Reuter which together handle a major proportion of the world's news. It does not have a combination of wealthy markets, private capital and government backing at its disposal. Nonetheless, it has dared to challenge both their domination of international information channels and their very news values by putting an alternative into practice.

IPS styles itself "an international non-profit cooperative of professional journalists, most of them from the third world". It aims to help reduce the information imbalance between wealthy and poorer nations by carrying more news about the third world from the perspective of third world countries themselves and by acting as a go-between for these countries to communicate with each other. And it has progressed far enough down this road to become the target of a campaign, led by some of the US commercial media apparently with some official backing from the US government. The campaign badly hurt its reputation and its budget.

Inter Press came into being in 1964 as a general news agency for Latin America. Its strongholds were the southern Cone countries, especially Argentina and Uruguay. Over the next ten years, in an atmosphere of growing radicalization in many parts of Latin America, the agency moved to the left. By the early-mid 70s, however, the forces of reaction had destroyed all chances of success for democracy in Bolivia, Uruguay, Chile and Argentina and many IPS correspondents fled into exile in Mexico and in Rome. The two founder-members of the agency, Italian journalist Roberto Savio (now Director General) and Argentinian Pablo Piacentini (now Editorial Director) had to find ways of giving IPS a new lease of life.

A logical and important gap to fill, they decided, was that of a third world news agency working for "the decolonization of information". Most IPS Latin American correspondents had observed at close quarters what it meant to have information carried in and out of their countries by the huge Western media conglomerates. Events reported tended to be those of interest to the US and leading

European countries, told from their perspective. Issues of underdevelopment and oppression and the people's organizations fighting them were often misrepresented or deemed "unnewsworthy". And third world journalists trained in the Western tradition took such news values as their model. Communications control by the big Western powers was perpetuating their political, economic and cultural control.

So as a third world news agency IPS began to branch out beyond its traditional strongholds of Latin America's southern Cone into Mexico and the Arab countries. The same concern to decolonize information was emerging, meanwhile, from another quarter.

In 1976 the Movement of Non-Aligned Countries within the United Nations started to demand a New International Information Order (later the New World Information and Communication Order or NWICO). A key part of the battle for a new international *economic* order, the Movement argued, was for the third world to win access to the necessary technology and training to control its own means of communication. Its self-reliance and cultural identity were at stake. An angry response built up in the Western camp. Unesco, the UN agency spearheading the debate, was turned into a forum for bitter international controversy which still rages on...

IPS staff were able to say with some justification that they were already working towards a new information order. The goals listed by Sean MacBride, the leading figure behind Unesco's report on the subject, matched their own. So its support for the NWICO became a major part of the Inter Press public profile.

The agency set about forging links with the Non-Aligned Movement, became a distributor for its News Pool and subsequently reached news exchange agreements with 30 national news agencies in third world countries. By 1982 it had grown into a $5 million a year operation with some 250 staff, with an international satellite-linked telecommunications system and with bureaux and correspondents in 60 countries. In news agency terms it rates only sixth in size, after AP, UPI, AFP, Reuter and Tass. Compared, though, with other non-profit "alternatives" in the communication field it has made the big league.

The Inter Press Rome headquarters, once the home of Italian aristocrats and, in the more recent past, of the Chilean embassy, has the same feel of decaying grandeur about it as the city's famous Colosseum down the road. Offices are lofty, lined with faded oil paintings. In reception, a row of prime ministers, snapped at Mexico's North-South summit, smile down from the wall on middle-aged men in suits arriving for a board meeting. In the news room a row of journalists type on modern visual display units under ancient chandeliers, sub-editing the day's news for distribution.

Director-General Roberto Savio travels around the agency network for a good part of the year. Apart from being a founder of the agency, he sports a whole string of credentials including that of Unesco information consultant, former head of the Italian government press office under President Moro and one-time director of Latin American news for the Italian state broadcasting service (RAI). The all-male board and executive of IPS include ex-ambassadors and lawyers. And the visitors' list for any given month reads like a "Who's Who" of UN chiefs, church dignitaries and media experts.

IPS is a non-profit cooperative registered in Italy, whose international activities are carried out through a wholly-owned company in Panama. Any surplus cash the agency makes must, by law, be ploughed back into its working capital.

Well-wishers, staff and former staff have the option of becoming members of the cooperative. Purchasing $500 worth of shares or more is the membership qualification, with each member entitled to one vote at the annual general assembly. The assembly elects an 11-person board of directors representative of those areas of the world where IPS is active, which then appoints the Director General and an executive committee.

Inter Press operates as a supplier of its own news and a technical distributor of other people's, the latter furnishing nearly a third of its revenue. News and features prepared by IPS correspondents are translated and subbed in Rome and transmitted in English and Spanish to subscribers via the agency's network of satellite teleprinter channels. (Some selected news items are also made available in Arabic, German, Portuguese and Swedish.)

On average, 15 per cent of the daily transmission consists of material originated by national news agencies with which IPS has news exchange agreements. This material carries the agencies' own credit lines. IPS correspondents also sometimes choose and adapt the stories they want from this source and the transmissions go out with a joint credit line of IPS and the originating agency.

Under the distribution part of the IPS operation, telecommunications services are made available to national news agencies and networks such as the Non-Aligned News Agencies Pool and ASIN, the Latin American and Caribbean news system. These users then exchange their own material among themselves.

The remainder of the operation is mainly taken up with special projects, the bulk of them in collaboration with United Nations agencies, church and development organizations. In partnership, for instance, with Unesco, IPS is distributing two women's feature services from Latin America and Africa on the role of women in development. In partnership with the International Foundation for Development Alternatives (IFDA) it produces a daily bulletin for diplomatic missions to the UN in New York, Geneva and Rome. And an IPS weekly service provides in-depth information on economic issues, agriculture, petroleum, minerals, environment and church affairs, bought by institutions and companies with a special interest in these different areas.

Close links with church organizations and the religious press have been built up by IPS in many parts of the world. In Geneva, for example, under a reciprocal agreement between IPS and the World Council of Churches, the WCC subscribes to the IPS service and the local IPS correspondent monitors the WCC for possible stories. About 12 per cent of the material published by the church news agency EPD in the Federal Republic of Germany is supplied by IPS and the local IPS representatives take part in the German Evangelical Church's discussions and activities centred on the New International Information Order.

Roughly a third of the 1981 income of $4,800,000 was generated by the sale of the news service to media subscribers and national news agencies. The technical distribution services earned another third while the rest came from a combination of the UN agreements and other special projects.

While material bought by the media brings in only a small fraction of total earnings, IPS points out that no international news agency supports itself from the sale of news alone. Reuter makes a substantial part of its income through its commercial and economic services. UPI leases out its telecommunications channels. Others depend on government subsidies, indirectly in the case of Agence France Press, directly in the case of most third world agencies.

The IPS "presence" in different parts of the world varies a lot. It may be one journalist and a teleprinter in a main city, as in Brazil. It may be a small office linked up with the national news agency of the country concerned, as in Cuba. It may be a team of people responsible for coordinating a whole region, as in Costa Rica, Jamaica, Mexico, Tunisia, Lebanon and Sri Lanka.

As demanded by its international outreach, Inter Press has always maintained offices in industrialized countries in Western and Eastern

Europe, the USSR and the USA. It also has agreements with a number of national news agencies in the industrialized world including Tanjug (Yugoslavia), EPD (Federal Republic of Germany), APA (Austria), ANP (Netherlands), MTI (Hungary), AGERPRESS (Romania), PAP (Poland), and ANOP (Portugal).

The strengths of IPS, in the eyes of subscribers and the agency itself, lie in its Latin American and Middle East coverage. Some headway is being made in establishing the agency in Asia and Africa but this has been hard going. Head of research, projects and training, Phil Harris, maintains that colonialism in these continents has produced media "much more in tune with those of the West".

Africa, Phil Harris pointed out, was also the world's poorest continent with the least developed communications infrastructure. "Many African countries are interested in exchanging news with us but can't afford it." Tanzania, he said, was a case in point. A telecommunications link between Dar-es-Salaam and Rome would cost Tanzania $20,000 a year — a considerable part of its entire information budget.

Despite network gaps like these, IPS believes it is making the grade as an "alternative news agency" on a world scale. It bases its claim firstly on the kind of news coverage it places and secondly on its role "as a vehicle for the voice of the third world".

IPS reporting is projected as people-oriented rather than celebrity-centred, dealing with issues as well as immediate events and including the necessary analysis to set news in the proper context. In addition, says IPS, it carries the voice of the third world countries by distributing the selected material from these countries' national news agencies along with its own reports and by putting its telecommunications channels at their disposal. All this has developed without any government subsidy and without the technical and service agreements being allowed "to compromise the professionalism and independence of (our) news service in any way".

How well do these claims stand up to closer scrutiny? Where editorial content is concerned, about half the daily output of Inter Press is the bread-and-butter product of all news agencies — "hard" news and news-based features. To be a credible operation, staff argue, you have to supply a certain amount of the same-day coverage carried on all the wires.

It is on this terrain that IPS competes most directly with the transnational and big European agencies in the mass media market place. As one staff member put it: "We're alternative in a very unalternative infrastructure."

Up to now the big press agencies have had a significant edge by being able to afford a regionalized, round-the-clock news service. This enables them to bridge the different time zones and meet evening copy deadlines in every part of the world. IPS material, transmitted 14 hours a day in Spanish and 10 hours in English, mostly from Rome, may arrive much later in some places, although plans are in the offing to expand and regionalize transmission.

"Even when IPS gets a 'scoop' the story isn't necessarily used by editors," explains former English Desk Editor, Peter Ford. Because the service was still not well enough known in some quarters, he said, editors were likely to sit on a controversial IPS story until they saw it carried later by other agencies.

The quality of news from local IPS correspondents is uneven as far as readability and the sourcing of material are concerned. It is also pitched most often at the level of national leaders and government-to-government dealings. Says Editorial Director Pablo Piacentini: "Lack of resources prevents us from doing as much social and grassroots coverage as we would like. It means a lot of work and is difficult to do from a capital city." The main difference between IPS and other agencies, he adds, is that IPS is conscious of that.

"Hard" news lends itself less readily than features to any kind of different treatment. And some of the national news agency material selected for inclusion in the daily transmissions has been criticized by users as turgid, superficial and full of government protocol.

Within limits, nonetheless, a departure from conventional news values by IPS's own correspondents is proving possible. In the case of the Pope's trip to Brazil IPS concentrated on his exposure to social problems rather than the ceremonial side of the visit. When the infant formula controversy blew up in the mid 70s about milk companies pushing their milk products in poor countries to the detriment of breast feeding, IPS news focused on the malpractice taking place and the international pressure on the companies it provoked.

IPS link person with the UN, Vic Sutton, points out the problems in giving news agency information any kind of direct advocacy function. "Unless we can generate some mass constituency of our own we have to work within a professional discipline." He argues that IPS correspondents do a useful job by reporting as widely and accurately as possible. News stories, too, were often a good lever for getting in-depth features into print.

News analysis and background material, including some of the development-related special services, make up approximately 40 per cent of Inter Press editorial output. As with news, subject matter is heavily weighted towards the international economy, national politics and development problems. Issues such as trade, technology, disarmament, health and education and the UN conferences which deal with them are looked at in critical detail from the point of view of their impact on the poorest countries in particular.

Articles about indigenous minority groups, and national liberation movements like SWAPO in Namibia and the Palestine Liberation Organization (PLO) report these movements' grievances and their fight for self-determination and not, as is more common, their disruptive effect on the existing order.

Just as great as the challenge of transcending traditional news values is getting this kind of news to readers. Because of the way they work none of the international news agencies have much control over how their material is used nor more than a rough idea of how many people they ultimately reach. The number of IPS readers is especially difficult to estimate since a chunk of its material goes out indirectly via national news agencies without IPS credit lines or is used by journalists as background information. "95 per cent of our work is a shot in the dark," say staff.

Building up media subscribers is more difficult than it has ever been, in a communications industry squeezed by world recession. When the budgets of many newspaper editors allow for subscriptions to only two or three agencies at the most, they are more likely to stay with the best-known ones. There is a solid core of non-media customers for IPS in the shape of solidarity committees, action groups, churches, education and research institutions and voluntary agencies. To succeed on its own terms, however, the organization must hold up as a *bona fide* news agency communicating not only to the "converted" but with a much wider audience via the mass media.

A recent progress report by IPS revealed that the agency's regular media subscribers number nearly 500, an apparently low figure even allowing for the "hidden" clients supplied indirectly via national news agencies. The same report argued: "Bearing in mind the number of countries served by IPS, and the weaknesses of the media in many third world countries, IPS's outreach is significant. However, much remains to be done, first to increase... subscribers, and second, to build revenues from media sales."

Indications are that in many third world countries, especially those in the American or British sphere of influence, the main newspapers tend to stick with the leading news agencies. At the same time, individual progressive editors and the more liberal papers find IPS material an asset. The editor of one such paper in the Dominican

Republic, Juan Bolivar Diaz of *El Nuevo Diario,* says: "What IPS lack in speed they make up for in depth of coverage on things like energy resources and oil — they have a third world view."

Argemiro Ferreira, foreign editor of the Rio de Janeiro daily, *Tribuna da Imprensa,* is convinced that one of the most dangerous aspects of US domination of the media in Brazil is that Brazilian journalists have absorbed the standards of the transnational agencies. IPS, on the other hand, has a third world perspective. "If we have IPS working here we can push the big papers. They can see that there are other kinds of stories."

Research among IPS media subscribers in industrialized countries has shown that the agency is valued for its background analysis and commentary, not for "hot" news. News stories are more often incorporated into other articles as one of several sources rather than being published in their entirety. Features used tend to be those on subjects like energy and environment which coincide with already existing interests in the West. Some radio stations as well as newspapers take material. Says the IPS office in Bonn, Federal Republic of Germany: "The press here is much more conservative than the radio which uses a lot of our stuff."

The heartland of the giant agencies, the USA, has not surprisingly proved tough for IPS to penetrate. Working through Interlink Press Service in New York, Inter Press is now launching feature "packages", translated and adapted in the US for the US market. Says an Interlink staff member involved: "Whether this can be done while staying faithful to the original (IPS) perspective has yet to be seen."

When Inter Press claims to promote "a larger third world voice in the international information system" through its technical distribution service, the "third world voice" is a network of national news agencies. Many of these, at least at this stage of their countries' development, are part of the state apparatus. As such, they can only reflect the real concerns and needs of the people in so far as their governments are addressing those needs. And some IPS telecommunications customers like Iraq, and former customer, the Shah of Iran, have paid scarce attention to internal democracy or human rights.

Guyana is another contradictory case. IPS furnishes the country with news, has given training to two journalists attached to its recently-launched national news agency, and carries the agency's own material on Inter Press distribution channels. Guyana is one of the most vocal advocates of a new international information order.

Yet the regime's repression of its opponents and its efforts to stifle independent media *internally* are well documented.

In a public statement published in May 1981, the People's Progressive Party slammed the traditional domination of the mass media in Guyana by transnational corporations. The statement was just as critical, however, of the ruling party's information policy. It went on to argue that "the concept of press freedom" has to be seen in the context of the class struggle, of which is the class in power, of who owns the mass media and for what purpose it is being used.

Separate credit lines distinguish stories by IPS correspondents from the "official-style" national agency material relayed as part of the technical distribution service. Research has shown, though, that the distinction inevitably gets blurred in the minds of some subscribers, posing something of a credibility problem.

While IPS stresses that it receives no government subsidies and can therefore keep its independence intact, dealing with governments, directly through distribution contracts and indirectly through the UN, is fundamental to its survival. This reliance produces its own constraints.

Some Inter Press journalists report that the importance of contracts with certain governments has at times obliged them to soft-pedal on incoming news items critical of these countries. Others, like the former director of the IPS London office, Phil Gunson, put the problem more strongly. "When I first joined Inter Press in 1978", he says, "the three big contracts were with Venezuela, Iraq and Libya. It was impossible for us to carry anything critical on those regimes."

The same issue of editorial constraints came up in a study of IPS completed in 1979 for the agency by the Peace Research Centre of Nijmegen University in the Netherlands. The study found that "a mechanism of self-selection cannot be denied", and mentioned cautious reporting of a non-aligned countries conference and of the oppression of Kurds in Iraq.

IPS chiefs argue that they would rather lose a contract — and did so for a while in the case of Libya — than allow a client to dictate the agency's news coverage. Reliance on a handful of important contracts has since shifted, they say, in favour of special projects like those with UN agencies which bring in 20 per cent of the annual turnover. But here again, constraints come into play. These agencies are themselves very dependent on governments (some rely on the US for 25 per cent of their funding) so Inter Press gets caught in the political crossfire. The recent US assault on the agency illustrates this point.

Led by several Western media organizations which were vigorously attacking Unesco and all exponents of the New International Information Order, it began in mid-1981. That was when the *Washington Star* ran an article attacking UN support for IPS on the ground that the agency was too pro-third world to be objective. The story was also distributed worldwide on Associated Press wires.

Further articles and accusations have charged IPS with being a partisan agency working against US interests, with secretly accepting funds from powers hostile to the US and with adopting a "standard anti-imperialist line". Out of its numerous news exchange agreements, IPS's links with the PLO and Libya have been singled out for special mention.

American state department officials subsequently instructed US embassies to vet any contract between IPS and the UN. Embassies should also use their influence, said officials, to block other prospective IPS agreements.

Quick to respond, Inter Press held meetings with its critics across the Atlantic, then went on to open its books to an independent investigation and audit. Later it was able to report: "Following discussions with IPS the US government has since accepted the agency's bona fides, and criticism from the US commercial media has been less frequent."

However a great deal of damage had already been done. The agency lost a number of contracts, found itself forced to carry out heavy pruning of projects and staff, and faced a serious cumulative deficit at the end of 1982. Several voluntary and church agencies among others have been approached to contribute towards aiding IPS's recovery so that present projects can be maintained and new ones launched as planned. New projects envisaged include a church-development network of journalists, a link-up of third world documentation centres, and news services in Dutch and Norwegian.

Before it embarks on many more projects, this could be an opportune moment for IPS to examine the contradictions and pressures it has encountered over the years. Individual staff and former staff see the direction it has taken very differently. Some say that between national news agency "propaganda" distributed and UN-related development material there is little room left for "genuine alternative news". Some say that news about development *is* part of the "alternative" news produced. Some say IPS was never supposed to be an "alternative" to the big agencies but complementary to them by offering analysis and background.

This crucial debate could benefit from a thorough airing among the staff as a body together with IPS's closest supporters. And the annual assembly of shareholders of the IPS cooperative seems the obvious place to do it. Yet though employees can buy shares in the cooperative and thereby be admitted to the assembly, there is no system of *automatic* staff representation on it and only about a third have joined as individuals.

Also, the real decision-making power, as the Netherlands study for IPS found, lies with the board and executive whose central figure is the Director General. "Thus (the) structure", said the report, "is apparently not much different from that of a 'normal', vertically organized concern."

Its vertical style of management was one of the charges levelled at IPS by the agency's now defunct London office. Relations between the Rome headquarters and the London staff deteriorated to such an extent that in 1981 IPS found itself locked in a dispute with the UK's National Union of Journalists (NUJ). A post-entry closed shop for staff was eventually negotiated. Summing up the dispute, the NUJ newspaper said that its officials "were at times confounded by the attitude of the company (Inter Press) which failed to comply with labour laws by not issuing contracts to people who worked for them regularly, and having recourse to lawyers."

Former IPS staff member, Pat Murray, who was NUJ shop steward in the London office at the time, makes a point from her perspective as a trade union activist about IPS news coverage. Even with the agency's third world specialization, she maintains that there is still scope for its reports from industrialized countries to focus far more on the actions of groups such as trade unionists, women and black people. "Their struggles are every bit as mutilated by the established media — and in a more sophisticated way." IPS's usual approach, she felt, was to concentrate on the policies of governments and transnational corporations insofar as they affect the fortunes of the third world.

IPS has clearly met one of its main goals of promoting news from countries which have previously fared badly in the world information flow. But it weakens its credibility by frequently describing the third world as if it were homogeneous and by implying that information from it or about it must be progressive *per se*. This fudges over some fundamental ideological issues and leaves IPS more vulnerable to attacks like that of the US which was, above all, ideological.

Where *content* rather than *flow* is concerned, it is debatable as to what point IPS is managing to meet its other main goal of transcending traditional news values. Its experience seems to raise the question as to whether any news agency operating in the present commercial and political structures can hope to achieve this to a significant extent.

# Community access –
# but for how long?

### Background

It was unheard of. The biggest TV station in the mid-south of the United States had been hauled before the Federal Communications Commission accused of serious broadcaster misconduct. A petition filed by the United Church of Christ (UCC) complained that WLBT-TV in Jackson, Mississippi, had discriminated against blacks, Jews and Catholics and promoted neo-Nazi organizations.

That was in 1964 and was only the start of a 15-year battle, led by the UCC, to make WLBT responsive to the needs of the black community. But the case made national headlines. And by establishing the right of the public to have a say in decision-making in broadcasting, it paved the way for today's media reform movement in the United States, fighting for public accountability and access.

Never has such a movement had its work more cut out than in the present US telecommunications boom. Satellites, data transmitters, computers and cable television arrived with the promise of revolutionizing communications — of offering tremendous openings for information and expression. Cable TV, especially, was heralded as a unique communications phenomenon and an ideal resource for local communities.

Unlike ordinary television which transmits through the air, cable TV picks up incoming signals through a control centre, usually from broadcast, microwave or satellite antennae, and retransmits them to viewers' homes through a cable.

The system was first started thirty years ago as a way of solving the problem of poor TV reception in hilly areas. Today it is a mushrooming $1.5 billion industry and promises to become the major means by which people in the US receive news, information, entertainment, and conduct their day-to-day transactions. In 1980 there were 4,200 cable systems in the US reaching about 15.1 million subscribers — 20 per cent of the nation's TV households. The industry reckons that the majority of US homes will be wired for cable within the next decade.

Cable came as a formidable challenge to America's three national broadcast networks, ABC (American Broadcasting Company), CBS (Colombia Broadcasting System), NBC (National Broadcasting Company), because of its special selling points. The three big networks have only one channel each, financed by advertising slotted into the programmes. Cable systems, on the other hand, offer a minimum of 12 channels and a maximum of 54, mostly uninterrupted by commercials, for a basic monthly subscription of $8.50.

Cable also presents the possibility, not yet fully operational, of two-way communication — of enabling people to record votes in opinion polls and to speak to each other from different places. When linked up to computers, cable systems make even more new services feasible. Viewers will soon be able to order groceries, place bets, buy plane tickets, make banking transactions, receive the latest news bulletins straight off the wires and have burglar and fire alarm systems — all via their TV screens.

Cable really took off as a lucrative mass medium in 1975 when Home Box Office (HBO), part of Time Inc., became the first of many programme suppliers to achieve nation-wide distribution to local cable operators by hiring part-use of an RCA (Radio Corporation of America) communications satellite. HBO also pioneered pay-cable, the system by which subscribers pay extra to receive programmes such as first run movies and sports, plus services like burglar alarms. Pay services can cost as much as $500 a year on top of the basic fee and are pushing up profits faster than ever. Industry revenues nearly doubled from $800 million in 1978 to $1.5 billion in 1980 of which $200 million was for pay cable.

The impact of cable on the life of the US churches has been dramatic. It has also been controversial, having highlighted some vastly different understandings about how mass communication connects with Christian ministry.

In the mid 70s evangelical fundamentalism emerged as an important religious, social and political force in the US and evangelical groups lost no time in taking advantage of the opportunities presented by cable. Their prominence in cable religious programming has left many mainline churches feeling outflanked.

The "electronic church" dominates cable's four satellite-fed religious networks, Christian Broadcasting Network (CBN), PTL (Praise the Lord) Television Network, Trinity Broadcasting Network and National Christian Network. At no extra charge to the cable subscriber or to the cable operator, the networks turn out round-the-clock-religion in the form of variety and chat shows, Bible studies, music programmes, counselling sessions and revival services.

The services have made household names of preachers like Moral Majority president, Jerry Falwell, Oral Roberts and Rober Schuller who finance their appearances on the screen with appeals for money which bring in millions of dollars. Falwell told a meeting of fundamentalist Christians in Dallas in 1980 that the "Bible belt" in America had become a "Bible cloak", beamed down on the country by satellite.

Satellite link-ups, however, come expensive as the National Christian Network discovered. To pay its way the Network sold off some of its satellite time to Playboy Enterprises to show adult films. A spokesperson explained to the press: "It's only an interim thing... it was either this or lose the entire ministry and be obligated for hundreds and thousands of dollars."

Since the early mid-70s the mainline churches have concentrated on helping their congregations around the country to take part in local cable TV programmes and put together religious prgrammes of their own. Some, parishes regularly videotape and "cablecast" worship services, religious plays and Christian education courses. Some, who share studios and equipment with other groups in the community, have been able to branch out into making religious magazine programmes and documentaries.

This approach of involvement at the community level comes a lot closer, the mainline denominations often say, to the essence of religious experience than the tub-thumping mass aproach of the electronic church. Nonetheless, the expansion of satellite link-ups with cable have opened up more tempting opportunities for the churches of establishing themselves on TV nation-wide. And some denominations appear to be backtracking on their earlier reservations about national programming.

The United Methodists, for example, the second largest US Protestant denomination with 9.5 million members, wanted to buy its own commercial TV station. Soaring costs eventually put the idea out of reach. Nonetheless, the church decided to press ahead with a massive campaign aimed at raising $25 million to build itself a national TV presence.

Not everyone in the denomination was happy about this scheme. Its opponents said that although a separate fund drive was supposed to take place so as not to drain central coffers, constituents had only a finite amount to give. The TV shows, it was feared, could therefore end up competing for money with other priorities of the church such as support for ethnic minority churches and projects to combat poverty. In the event, the scheme is being scrapped for fear of overstretching the church's resources.

In another ambitious financial venture, more than 70 of the 171 Catholic dioceses in the US have joined a National Catholic Telecommunications Network set up by the US Catholic Conference in 1981. The Network uses satellite to beam religious programming to the participating dioceses which, in turn, offer the programming to their local cable systems.

By contrast, religious programming accounts for only a tiny fraction of the numerous activities of the United Church of Christ in relation to cable, and to broadcasting in general. The UCC, says its office of communication, understands its mandate as helping "to see that everyone is given an equal opportunity to work in, be covered fairly by, and have access to, the resources of telecommunications".

For instance, the UCC challenges individual radio and TV stations like WLBT in Jackson, Mississippi, about their racism or unwillingness to air opposing viewpoints. It advises minorities and women on how to break into cable, as employees and as systems owners. It defends the right of developing countries to have access to satellite frequencies.

The church believes that its education scheme on cable is the only one of its kind being offered in the country outside universities. The plan embraces an extensive programme of workshops around the country designed to teach church and community leaders, trade unionists and minority groups how cable works and how they can get the most from it by creating their own programming. For 1982-84 the budget for the workshops is $350,000, of which $50,000 has been committed by the UCC and the rest by outside donors.

A policy declaration by the UCC office of communication in 1981 spells out its theological understanding of its ministry and mission in communications. Discipleship, said the declaration, called Christians both to proclaim the gospel and to act upon the imperatives which it contains. Therefore, the communication effort of the UCC required both telling and doing. "As part of its ministry to its constituency and the world, the denomination is responsible for communicating the 'good news' of the church and its activities. But it has also committed itself to a mission in and to the mass communication media, a mission which is founded on the biblical mandates of teaching, stewardship and justice." The UCC's education work, the statement went on, was in response to the "teaching" mandate. The fight for fair coverage and public access was based on the mandate of "stewardship". The advocacy of fair treatment in the communications field for the disadvantaged and disenfranchized came from the "justice" mandate.

Programming efforts of churches at local level often cross-fertilize with the lively citizens' access movement in the US. Successful action on access tends to be patchy because cable is regulated primarily by states and cities rather than by the federal government, and access is therefore a matter of negotiation between municipalities and individual cable operators. Still, where the agreed franchise *does* call on the cable operator to provide access channels for the local community, cable has turned teachers, nurses, students, elderly citizens and clergy into TV producers. In 1979, according to the UCC, 400 communities were regularly producing access programmes. By 1982 there were many more, plus 600 access centres spread across the country.

Non-profit organizations like the National Federation of Local Cable Programmers (NFLCP) act as a clearing house for users of local channels to swap ideas and experiences. The NFLCP also runs conferences and advises communities how to lobby their city councils when franchizing for cable comes up. It helped to draft a "model" franchizing code for cities' guidance and it is also fighting moves at Congress level to make access illegal.

Dr George Stoney, Professor of TV and Film at New York University and a founder of NFLCP, is known as the father of the video access movement. He believes that, despite its uneven development, the movement has gone from strength to strength. He lists a string of examples to prove it — community cable-casting by Chicanos in Muskataine, elderly citizens in Iowa, schools, colleges, hospitals, youth clubs.

Of the churches George Stoney says: "Cable has been used by (them) in all kinds of ways; by preachers to make a name for themselves, as a public relations gimmick and as a tool of evangelism." Christians could be so bedazzled by the mechanics of the medium, and so concerned about building the churches, that they sometimes forgot what the church stood for.

One group which hasn't made this mistake and which sums up, in his view, what the video access movement is all about, is St John's Community Video Centre in Knoxville, Tennessee, known as "Channel 20".

### The church that made cable a community resource

The weekly round-up of religious news is being read by Cornelia Hickman, a sunny, middle-aged woman who helps out in the office. She studies her script, waiting for the go-ahead from her crew, Melinda Foster on camera and Gerald Valentine on sound. Noise is proving a problem since they are recording in the only free space available that afternoon, the church car park.

Next door, in the wing of the parish house-cum-TV centre, a black band from Nashville, in town to do a benefit concert for the people of El Salvador, is warming up in the studio. Around the rota blackboard, clusters of volunteers work out their schedules for future programmes. A local elections candidate rings through, asking when he can come in to be interviewed...

It has been that kind of week at Channel 20, a small cable television station in Knoxville, Tennessee.

Knoxville nestles in conservative "Bible belt" territory in the south-east of the United States. A well-heeled, law-abiding, manufacturing town of 183,000 people, its only claim to fame until recently was its proximity to the Great Smoky Mountains National Park and the atomic city of Oak Ridge. Then came the news that Knoxville would host the 6-month-long World's Fair in 1982. And in the spring of that year, as Cornelia began her car park news programme, the town was standing by, its buildings repainted, its roads resurfaced and its string of new hotels at the ready, to receive the US President and a predicted 13 million visitors.

Channel 20 is Knoxville's only community cable station and, according to many media campaigners, one of the few public access centres of its kind in the country. It became a possibility when a cable operator put in a bid to wire Knoxville and agreed to set aside one of the system's 12 active channels for community use. It became a reality because there was a far-sighted church ready to make sure that the chance didn't go to waste.

St John's Episcopal Church, a prestigious marble edifice in downtown Knoxville with a prosperous congregation to match, was already videotaping its worship service when cable came along. Minister Dan Matthews argued that St John's should back Knoxville's public access effort in cash and in kind as part of its city-centre ministry. He convinced the congregation even though, because the city was wired on only a small scale at first, most church members couldn't yet see what they were supporting.

From the moment St John's Community Video Centre opened its doors in 1975 and began cable-casting on Channel 20, the church regarded it as a community resource and "only incidentally" as an outlet for religious programming.

That "open space" policy still stands. All Channel 20's programmes are devised and produced by local people themselves with the help of four paid staff. It is the place where, if a group can make a case for a programme of interest to the community, they can do it — whether or not they have any previous TV experience and whether or not they have any church connection. "I couldn't believe you could just walk in and do a programme," says Melinda Foster.

Cable-casting nine hours a day Monday to Friday and two hours on Sunday to a potential audience of 70,000 cable subscribers, Channel 20 has grown to a point where it sustains twenty regular programmes and a pool of over 150 volunteers.

In any given week the Centre's neatly kept studio, transmissions room and office are usually buzzing with people. They are white, black, young, middle-aged and elderly, women and men, Christians and people of other faiths. They may be businessmen from the "Toastmasters'" public speaking society, students from the university's communications course, doctors' wives planning their "healthline" programme, the local stargazer doing his astronomy-made-easy spot...

All groups go through four basic training sessions in a friendly atmosphere which soon dispels the notion that only experts can make TV programmes. Merikay Waldvogel, former director of the Knoxville Women's Centre, remembers how she and others were taught to tackle programmes on women's issues. "Instead of freaking out in front of a camera many of us really gained self-confidence. It was very positive and creative to be learning new skills together."

When a young Canadian woman who was blind turned up and asked to learn, staff were as determined as she was that her disability shouldn't stop her. Now Penny Zibula hosts a popular weekly talk programme about people and events in Knoxville, cued to begin and end the show with a string tied to her right ankle.

"We try to help groups without making them too dependent on us," say the staff. General manager Peggy Gilbertson and 26-year-old programming director David Rutledge used to be volunteers themselves. Peggy was one of a group of doctors' wives who wanted to do a health information programme. David, from Delaware, worked in various parts of the country after college and came in one day looking for the chance to pick up some creative and socially useful skills.

Jonathan Hardin, in charge of crews, used to work for one of the big TV network affiliates until he tired of making so many commercials. Tommy Gibbons, 23, in charge of editing, arrived on a student placement and became so involved that he returned when his exams were over.

Occasionally there are disappointments when a volunteer uses the training as a career stepping stone rather than making a commitment to the station. Many drop out, as well, after they realize the amount of time and hard work involved. Others, though, plough back in what they've learned many times over. They receive further training, stand by to supplement crews, and pass on their skills willingly to newcomers.

One of these is Tom Simpson, a member of the church and local teacher who trained with Channel 20 when it first started and still crews for the St John's Sunday morning worship programme. He has taught children at his school how to video their basketball games and make some of the educational programmes carried by the cable system.

Another "regular" is Gerald Valentine, the janitor for a neighbouring church. He first walked in when he was an unemployed Vietnam veteran with a broken marriage and too much time on his hands. Channel 20, he says, not only gave him a new interest, it was a "life-saver" for him, bringing him new self-esteem and the will to put his life back together.

A quarter of the volunteers' output consists of music programmes — jazz, gospel, country, blue grass, symphony and choral. Another sizeable chunk concentrates on the nitty-gritty of local life such as craft-making, schoolboy boxers, "Cooking with Tony" and children's plays produced by elementary schools from all over the city.

Still other programmes provide straightforward community information. "Healthline" deals with medical problems in everyday language and from the patient's perspective, while talk shows discuss facilities available for the elderly, the disabled, the young, the unemployed.

Issue-oriented programmes also have their place. Studio debates on abortion, drugs, rape or child abuse have received "educational rather than sensational" treatment and featured local people directly affected as well as "experts". One Channel 20 helper volunteered to speak on the drugs programme about her own family trauma. She is the mother of a youth imprisoned on drug offences.

Students from a local college showed their video about dangerous working conditions in Tennessee's coal mines on Channel 20. The programme, which consisted of interviews with wives and workmates of miners who had been killed or injured, illustrated the exploitation of coal miners in no uncertain terms.

The station has mainly steered clear, as Tommy Gibbons puts it, "of the money and glamour aspect" of the World's Fair. It chose instead to focus on the plight of an estimated 2,000 people forced to move out of their homes so that landlords could re-rent their apartments to Fair visitors at inflated prices. Gerald Valentine was among the tenants affected and led a protest of his neighbours to a city inquiry. He also made an unexpected TV appearance on another channel when, within sight of a film crew, he lost his cool and chased his landlord round the block!

The responsibility of providing community access to local government is taken very seriously at Channel 20. It is the only station to cablecast "live" the whole of the city council meetings ("deadly to watch at times but they show the workings of a political system and often how the system doesn't work").

It is also the only station which gives each of the candidates in the local elections a free seven-minute interview spot to put forward her/his position — all 103 of them! Whenever another candidate arrives at the studio to be interviewed, David Rutledge emerges in jeans and T-shirt, does a lightning change into a suit and sprints round with his clipboard in front of the camera.

Religious programming, kept to 10 per cent of the total ouput as a matter of policy, is a very ecumenical business. The Sunday service from St John's is a regular feature as is the very different First Apostolic Church service with its drums and choirs. But for the rest, crews are encouraged to steer clear of the preaching format in an effort to interest a wider spectrum of viewers. Recent offerings have included slave songs from visiting Georgia musicians, dramatic monologues on the lives of the apostles and overseas stories from former missionaries.

Channel 20 emphasizes that it is not trying to compete on the same terms as the three big networks and the 11 other cable channels received by households in the area. Quality-wise, staff achieve a generally high standard despite the lack of resources, but feel that ultimately, giving people the chance to make programmes is more important than how good (or bad) those programmes turn out to be.

Nor are they overly preoccupied by viewing figures. The fact that there are 12 cable channels altogether going out to 28,000 households suggests that Channel 20's audience share could be pretty modest. "Yes," says Dan Matthews, "it's a narrow ghetto channel, but that's its appeal and its strength."

Staff and volunteers all believe that they are providing a healthy alternative to the general American TV diet of movies, soap operas and advertizing, by covering subjects that are more local and in greater depth than commercial stations would spend the time and money to do. The soap operas, it is felt, also tend to reinforce stereotypes of women and minorities. Community TV on the other hand can help to overcome these. The Knoxville Women's Centre programme on women in non-traditional jobs was one example on Channel 20. A programme made by a black crew about the town's black community, its music, its bars, its businesses, etc., was another.

Interference in the content of programmes made by Channel 20 crews is almost unheard of. Tom Tucker, a church steward and chairperson of the church/TV liaison committee in charge of the station, says: "We will not censor anything if opinions on both sides of a question are represented." So long as groups accept this framework they are taken on trust. Staff don't even see beforehand everything that goes out on the station.

When James Sanders took over from Dan Matthews in 1981 as minister of St John's he inherited a TV station which couldn't claim to have drawn in more church members, whose staff didn't belong to St John's and many of whose volunteers probably didn't regard what they were doing as anything to do with religion at all. Nevertheless, for James Sanders as for his predecessor, Channel 20 is a legitimate and essential mission. It provides information for the community unavailable on the networks and shows that the fundamentalist theology of the electronic church is not the only theology on offer. Says James Sanders: "(The revivalists) have got a lot more viewers than we have but we're showing in a small way a viable alternative to that kind of Christian broadcasting."

There are plenty of signs that Channel 20 has established its credentials in the eyes of the community. The local evening paper, *The Knoxville News-Sentinel,* wrote in 1981: "(This) small television station is becoming a national model for developing community cable TV stations." The University of Tennessee and nearby Knoxville college send their communications students along to St John's to get some practical experience. A local hospital uses some of the "Healthline" tapes in the training of its student nurses. Another TV channel handed down a piece of its camera equipment. A concerned viewer phoned in about the aquarium used as a standard interlude scene. "Your fish aren't making many bubbles," he said, "they're not getting enough air."

For all its achievements, Channel 20 is not without problems. Paradoxically, though the church was its founder and has always been its main means of survival, there is little contact between the station and the majority of people in the congregation, and there are fewer church volunteers than earlier on. Church member Tom Simpson's opinion is that church volunteers have not been made to feel part of the project over recent years. General manager Peggy Gilbertson, on the other hand, feels most church members don't care and that she is therefore "out on a limb". And Tom Tucker with a foot in both camps concedes: "Our biggest disappointment is that more of the congregation are not involved. Many have not bought the (mission) idea."

The problem is accentuated by a lack of collective working and decision-making on the part of the overstretched and low-paid staff. "We're too busy to communicate with each other," says Jonathan Hardin. Also for the first time, the staff explain, the station is reaching a point where there are more people wanting to make programmes than there are resources available, and some hard choices will have to be made. "We need to be clearer about what purpose we are serving."

Until now the station has been responding to requests rather than initiating programme ideas. Jonathan believes it will be good to be forced to be more selective. The staff had sometimes not been discriminating enough, he felt, and had allowed programmes in which local people put in a plug for their own businesses. David Rutledge feels that staff and crews should go out more into the community and keep their ears to the ground for the most important issues. "We've a lot more responsibility to show people something they can't get somewhere else. That would give us a good reputation for being interested and active."

Everyone agrees that Channel 20 shouldn't stand still, only, as Jonathan says: "It's difficult because we don't have any models to follow."

Recent financial set-backs have made the station even more dependent on the church. When a government programme which was paying the salaries of two staff stopped its grant as part of the economic cut-backs, the church picked up the bill. Its regular commitment is already $27,000 a year — about 10 per cent of all pledges — while the premises, lighting, heating, etc. are probably worth half as much again.

Together with $20,000 a year from the city of Knoxville, and the occasional local grant for a specific series of programmes, Channel 20 struggles on. The equipment, in the meantime, is getting older. "Most of it is held together by chewing gum and masking tape. We need about $100,000 to re-equip."

Under the terms of the city franchise, the cable company, Athena, undertook to provide a fully equipped studio for its public access channel. In the event St John's came along instead, but the company never gave any money in lieu of providing the studio. Says Peggy Gilbertson: "It has done the bare minimum." Only now, after renewed pressure from the station and the city, was it considering a donation of $20,000 a year.

Although Athena is keeping eight unused channels for the time when pay cable and satellite-distributed programmes come to be more in demand, it has made no move to try to recover its access station. Channel 20 workers, in any case, believe that they have proved themselves as a public service and that the city would not allow the cable company to take the station back. Also, they point out, the franchise has another seven years to run.

Only if Congress decides to remove access from the jurisdiction of the municipalities could the picture change dramatically. Says Dan Matthews: "Should Federal laws take away the cities' bargaining power we're in trouble. The day a local franchise is not granted by the locality all my dreams of local TV are doomed."

**Uncertain future for cable users**

It is easy to understand why community programming enthusiasts point to Channel 20 as an example of what can be done. But the St John's experience is only part of the story. Local groups often find it hard to take advantage of access even if they can get hold of channel space on cable.

Cable companies are not obliged to provide any studio facilities, equipment or training for them unless it is written into the terms of the franchise. Making programmes is therefore a costly affair, involves learning technical skills and demands a great deal of time.

Unless reasons for getting involved are clearly worked out from the start, many people fall by the wayside when the novelty wears off. In fact, in some places access is in danger of fading away because it is under-used.

The quality and content of access programmes produced is another issue. While some are imaginative efforts to tackle subjects that wouldn't be a commercial proposition for the big networks, others are little more than second-rate imitations of mainstream programmes. Part of the problem, thinks Jane Baron who directs the workshop scheme of the UCC, is that groups often tend to regard getting access as an end in itself. "We try to help them to think through what they want to say," she explains.

Lesley Page-Brown, UCC coordinator for cable activities, underlines that local access programmes are also, by definition, only able to interest a very limited audience. "What really sells cable are movies and burglar alarm systems. Given a choice between burglar alarms and local programming, many people would choose burglar alarms."

The users of access at this stage are community groups of professional people, and to a much lesser extent trade unionists and pressure groups. Concerns of the poorer sections of society may be raised on cable in what George Stoney calls "advocacy by the middle class", but rarely by those people themselves. Nor do disadvantaged people get the chance to influence the industry from the inside. On minorities and women, for example, the UCC reported in 1981 that: "There is no indication from the employment statistics that the cable companies are making serious and strenuous efforts to recruit, hire and upgrade (them)."

Overall trends in the cable industry, however, may ultimately pose the biggest problem for the survival of ventures like Channel 20, and the creation of others like it. With cable, what began as promising local medium has become a mass phenomenon and with big profit appeal.

The result is that individual cable systems and small companies are being gobbled up by major corporations with necessary capital to invest in programmes, equipment and satellite services. Many of them like Time Inc., General Electric, Westinghouse and Warner Brothers are firms with massive interests in other branches of the electronics or media industries already. The time is fast approaching when cable, far from offering a greater choice, could carry news, information and entertainment entirely determined by a handful of the largest corporations.

All the signs are that the firms in cable will continue to offer access so long as the war to win city franchises is still on. But once secure, they will try to squeeze it off their channels at the first opportunity and fill up with as many programmes and services that people will pay for. Says Jane Baron: "If (access) doesn't make money for them it's a liability."

This trend is being borne out in many places, explains Dave Pomeroy, director of media resources for the National Council of Churches. "Seventy per cent of the total number of cable systems are 21-20 channel systems filled to capacity and with not much access," he says. Original hopes for genuine public access with cable had been realized "only to a very very limited extent".

George Stoney quotes Central Long Island, New York, where 36 out of the 37 channels on the cable system are given over to programmes made outside the area. All the rest — public information, education, etc. — is crammed into the one remaining channel, with local community programming awarded the princely total of two-and-a-half hours a week!

At the very time when regulations might have helped to protect the public interest, these are in danger of disappearing. In 1979 a Supreme Court ruling threw out the possibility of the Federal Communications Commission mandating access channels, leaving cities to bargain with cable systems operators as best as they could.

Now there is a bill pending in congress which would make it illegal for cities to insist on access as a condition of granting a franchise to a cable company. The bill is being backed in Washington by the powerful and well-off National Cable TV Association which represents the cable industry lobby.

For George Stoney none of these developments can detract from what has already been achieved. "We used to be completely dominated by the mass media," he says. "At least we have had ten years where we have seen what we can do ourselves." The main hope for the future, he feels, lies in rapidly educating more local communities who do not yet have cable about what is at stake when franchizing comes up, and in getting more people to take full advantage of existing access space. This would show Congress that there was a strong public lobby defending access and fighting de-regulation.

For Dr Everett Parker, director of the United Church of Christ office of communication, future prospects for access can't be seen in isolation from the wider political situation in the US. In a speech before the Tenth Annual Telecommunications Policy Research Conference in 1982 he made the case that the early media reform movement, born of the activist era of civil rights confrontations, anti-Vietnam protests and women's liberation campaigns in the early 60s, was now operating under much tougher conditions. Media reformers were finding their energies and resources fragmented by new and pressing economic, political and social issues. "It is hard", Parker said, "to see the vital need to keep the media open to public access and free of monopoly control when we are in a desperate struggle to save our jobs, put food on the table and stave off a macho drive for nuclear war."

The Reagan government, in line with its economic policies, was condoning monopoly in the guise of free enterprise and favoured the de-regulation of the telecommunications industry, Parker argued. "Unless we move quickly to stop de-regulation and to have consumer protection legislation passed," he went on, "the communications revolution will take place with the American people as its victims rather than its masters."

# Liberating the airwaves

### Background

Italy's showcase town of Bologna faced an all-out insurrection. Young workers, immigrants and students, angered by unemployment, soaring food prices and scarcity of decent, low-cost housing, took to the streets in a massive demonstration.

At first, the demonstrators' knack of evading police puzzled the authorities. Then they discovered that all the telephone kiosks at particular vantage points were occupied by callers relaying information to the local independent radio station which was broadcasting it back to the demonstrators. The station workers weren't just reporting the insurrection, they were coordinating it!

The story of Bologna's Radio Alice, silenced for its role in this 1977 uprising, is now something of a legend in Italy's socialist movement. In fact, independent radios were mushrooming throughout Italy at this time, turning established notions of mass communication on their heads, and on a scale never before experienced in Western industrialized society.

In the early 70s a handful of independent radio and TV stations started operating in the country, only to be shut down by police. The Italian state, it seemed, was destined to keep its stranglehold on broadcasting intact. Then came an unexpected constitutional court ruling in 1976. It found that independent radios and TV, as long as they were local, were also legal. The government's monopoly was about to give way to an astonishing broadcasting explosion.

Within just a couple of years Italy had nearly 3,000 "free" radios and over 500 TV stations, outflanking even the USA in stations per head of population. Still today, the total number of independent, public and foreign stations reaching Italian listeners makes this broadcasting system easily the most crowded in the world.

Free radio, being simpler and cheaper to set up than TV, took off in a bigger way at first. At one point (1977) Milan alone claimed 112 radios and Rome 110. A Rome hotel on the hilly outskirts of the city won unexpected fame for having a flat roof that bristled with transmitters of local radios competing to be heard.

Generally speaking the free radios are either commercial stations, radios owned by political parties or cooperatively run socialist stations. All of them, especially commercial radios, broadcast a lot of music, and nearly all are financed, wholly or partly, from advertizing.

Their arrival brought all kinds of innovations. It gave birth to the "phone-in", enabling people to exchange views and experiences without the need of a studio. It produced endless permutations of news, features, counter-information and political comment. Some called it chaos, others an exciting breakthrough. Everyone agreed broadcasting in Italy could never go back to what it was.

Developments in the Italian mass media have always gone hand in hand with political changes. After the Second World War when the Christian Democratic Party (CD) took over from Mussolini's fascists, it soon dominated the public broadcasting corporation, Radio Audizioni Italiana (RAI), as it dominated every other sector of the Italian state apparatus.

Eventually, after the Socialist Party entered the government coalition in 1968 and other parties began demanding their slice of airtime too, a campaign to reform RAI did come to the surface. Nontheless, it made little immediate headway and deadening uniformity prevailed, in the press as well as in broadcasting.

This was surprising, in a sense, given Italy's deep-rooted socialist traditions. The wartime resistance movement and the bitter onslaught against fascism had produced strong workers' organizations, the largest Communist Party in Western Europe and a leftist culture far broader than the Party itself. Yet it was a socialist movement without a powerful public voice.

An important factor was that the Communist Party, having been elbowed out of a part in government after the war, was forced to settle, until the 1976 elections, for influence at the regional level through its control of a number of key city councils like Bologna. So although it published its own newspaper, it failed to penetrate the mass media nationally to any great degree, and other socialist groups had even less success.

The big broadcasting shake-up changed all that, all the more so because it coincided with a new, fast-growing mass movement led by women, youth, students and young workers which overtook the Communist Party and made the political running through most of the 70s. Triggered by the general strike of May 1968 in France, this movement soon began to produce its own newspapers, books, poetry and songs. And it was to take full advantage of the new-found freedom of the airwaves by inventing the socialist radios.

These radios have never exceeded 35 per cent of the total. Nevertheless they have attracted worldwide attention. More than just a local, spontaneous, participatory version of the state broadcasting body, they are based on a whole different understanding of what communication is *for*. Extracts from a list of aims drawn up by Radio Città Futura in Rome spell this out:

1. To combat, on the terrain of daily information and culture, the operation of the dominant class through the major media...
2. ... to give voice to the issues raised in social struggles that aim not merely to transform the economic relations of production, but which also set themselves intermediate aims such as direct intervention in the fields of culture, the urban setting, patterns of leisure activity, the neighbourhood, education, etc.
3. To provide a reference point in the information field for those mass movements (women, students, unemployed) which do not possess their own means of communication... this means to link up the voices of these new forces, without any filtering process, with the overall mesh of social forces at work in society.
4. To produce information laterally, based on a type of mass relation to the city and national social life, which involves the people themselves, as transforming their role from ordinary passive consumers into active subjects in the work of the radio station...

Radio Città Futura, operating along these lines until 1979, was a collective whose public decision-making assemblies attracted anything up to 200 people at one stage. Other socialist radios may be just a few people, a turntable and a microphone. Some serve as a political mouthpiece of a particular group. Some take a completely "open space" approach offering airtime to organizations in the community.

But large or small, slick or crude, they constitute a mass phenomenon through which ordinary people have learned to express their needs and share information — the homeless, the jobless, factory workers, women, youth, gays... Issues usually downplayed by the mainstream media, like corruption in high places, fascist activity and police brutality came to be openly discussed on radio for the first time. So too did "taboo" subjects in Catholic Italy such as sexuality, divorce, contraception, abortion and drugs.

That this trend was seen as a threat in some quarters became all too clear. A worker with a station in Sicily was murdered a few days after naming a prominent mafia member on the air. In 1979, five Rome women from Radio Donna broadcasting a programme on contraception were machine-gunned in the legs and genitals by a group of masked fascists who broke into the studio.

Today the number of independent radios remains roughly the same — in 1981 around 2,800 with 8.2 million listeners. The proportion of socialist radios, however, has shrunk to 8 per cent. Rising costs and the need, given intense competition, to lay out huge sums of money for more powerful transmitters, has worked to the advantage of big corporations. Media magnates dominate both independent TV and radio, mopping up 26.6 billion lire* in radio advertizing revenue in 1981.

Promises of plurality have evaporated: the choice of programmes compared with the total number of stations broadcasting is extremely limited. TV stations offer mainly second-rate entertainment and old films, some pornographic, while commercial stations, on average, play music 70 per cent of the time.

The socialist radios, always dependent on committed volunteers or workers willing to give their help for subsistence pay, obviously find it a struggle to survive in this cut-throat commercial climate. When they were part of a movement which they supported and which supported them it was a different matter. In the event, by the end of the 70s that movement had become dispersed and demoralized.

The economic recession has since deepened. The rise of urban terrorism has been used by the government to discredit socialism in general and exercise repression against the left. Workers and social activists at all levels are on the defensive.

Thus the few who continue to use radio in Italy for something other than making money do so under very different conditions from

---

* One US dollar = Lit. 1,350.

the heady early days. They must settle, during these lean times, for providing a service where they can.

Even so, the experience they have been part of and are still pioneering has created far-reaching effects. At a general level, no one in Italy any longer questions whether independent broadcasting is legitimate, only how it can be rationalized. Then, within that, the very existence of an alternative socialist source of information has meant that censorship and bias in the mass media, though still in evidence, are no longer possible to the same extent as before. It is also worth noting that the state broadcasting body has launched a third TV channel with regional units which goes some way to treating the kind of local and minority issues first covered by the socialist radios. Above all, the socialist radio experience has informed the efforts of many inside and outside Italy who go on fighting for radical change in their societies and want to use communication as an instrument in that process.

## Lively forum for Milan's broad left

One morning in March, the regular phone-in and music programme of Milan's best-known socialist radio, Radio Popolare, is going out over the air. At the microphone talking to callers is a young woman in her twenties and another some ten years older.

It is the fourth anniversary of the assassination by the Red Brigades of Italy's former prime minister Aldo Moro. Callers have already spoken about this, about the current situation in El Salvador, and about the growing incidence of torture in some countries.

Now, on a different note altogether, the conversation shifts to sexuality. A man on the line talks about masturbation and the unnecessary guilt he thinks it causes. "People believe it's dangerous," he says, "but it's not true." Another caller complains: "My husband wants me to be more sexy." "Men's idea of how we women should look is conditioned by how the magazines show us," responds someone else. "It affects our own view of ourselves, too," suggests the elder programme presenter...

Upstairs in the radio's newsroom a battered telex machine disgorges the day's events so far and four journalists at their typewriters assemble the 12.30 news broadcast. Important stories expected later include a pensioners' demonstration in Rome and the threat of 4,000 redundancies at a Milan car factory.

When labour correspondent Dario Carella comes back from a meeting at the factory everyone quickly adjourns to the café across the road to hear what he has to say. Instead of interpreting the meeting, Dario has tape-recorded a chunk of the workers' actual discussions — rude remarks and all. To the amusement of other café customers he proceeds to play back an extract there and then. Back at the radio, within the hour, trade unionists all over Milan will hear the car workers rejecting the redundancy proposal, calling for solidarity action to help them fight it, and slamming their union leaders for being prepared to give in.

Since Radio Popolare (People's Radio) was started in 1976 by five workers from another left-wing station, it has coped with continual struggles to stay afloat. To hold their own in the radio "war", staff explain, they have been forced to step up their transmitter power from 400 to 5,000 kilowatts. Their running costs have rocketed from 60 million lire a year to 165 million in 1981. Sometimes they have had to choose between paying themelves or paying the phone bill. And they have long since outgrown their premises, a cramped, three-storey terraced house where visitors and volunteers jostle each other in the hallway and people dash up and down the narrow staircase between the offices, studio and record library on the ground floor, the news department on the second and the recording and editing rooms up top.

Yet Radio Popolare is regarded as the success story of Italy's independent left radios. Its broadcasts, on two frequencies, can be picked up within a 30-mile radius of the city and it claims 70,000 regular listeners a day plus 100,000 who tune in at least once a week.

Some of its programmes are re-broadcast by six free radios in the Lombardy region. Its paying supporters, who take out low-priced membership as a way of contributing to its income, number 10,000. Its mailing list of people who give donations and patronize fund-raising events contains 50,000 names.

Popolare is a station which not only carries news, but makes it. In 1978, after two young Milanese community workers had been murdered in the street by a fascist gang, the radio campaigned for a strike on the day of the funeral and 100,000 people in the city stopped work. In 1981 it was the only media channel to expose and denounce the torture of political prisoners in Milan's San Vittore jail, reading out letters over the air from the prisoners themselves and interviewing their families.

Unlike many other independent left radios in Italy, past and present, Radio Popolare sees itself neither as a mouthpiece which anyone in the socialist *milieu* can spontaneously make use of, nor as a platform for left organizations to address the activists in their particular orbits. Says the station's chairperson, Frederico Pedrocchi: "We are searching for a new kind of communication."

Popolare aims to provide the broadest possible forum where members of the socialist public at large can express themselves and communicate with each other. Such a socialist public is clearly visible in Milan. The city has a council with a majority of Socialist Party (SP) and Communist Party (CP) members, a militant, unionized labour force and a political culture to the left of most other main towns in Italy.

The radio's founders thought it important to ask for the blessing of the SP and CP which send representatives to the station's consultative Council of Administration, as a sign of formal recognition. Similarly the metalworkers union federation (FIM) gave its public backing, and still does.

To provide their popular forum and successfully create lateral mass communication outside existing channels, Radio Popolare's founders decided that they had to be professional about it. This meant having a core of experienced full-time workers, explained Michele Cocuzza, head of news. "Radio is a hot medium," he says. "We thought it was necessary to know this medium."

Michele Cocuzza and a nucleus of other journalists and students who launched the radio were all active in the new mass movement of the 70s. Since 1976 their collective has grown to thirty full-time writers, office workers and technicians, most of whom take a turn at the microphone at some stage of the week. They pay themselves 400,000 lire a month (about a third of the going rate for journalists), and organize themselves into teams dealing with different categories of programmes — news, culture, work, youth, education, etc. They elect their team heads, the editor-in-chief, and the chairperson who acts as overall coordinator and public spokesperson of the radio.

At meetings three or four times a month the full-time core group consults with the various representatives from the community sitting on the radio's Council of Administration. However the policy of the station and its day-to-day running rests with the collective which in turn consults with the numerous volunteer-collaborators working on programmes.

Programmes go out 24 hours a day, all of them prepared with a local audience in mind though few are simply local in scope. News and news-based features, for instance, deal with events in Milan, Italy and abroad.

Programmes produced by and for special interest groups, like the mid-afternoon "youth hour", are one type of regular transmission. Information features offer legal, health and other kinds of advice. Cultural programmes broadcast reviews and music. Public service announcements tell what's on, who has what for sale, and which are the best-value shops, bars and restaurants. Then there are the discussions and phone-ins, touching on everything from personal problems to the state of the world.

In spontaneous moments late at night the radio sometimes brings in hilarious innovations. It has watched TV with listeners with the sound switched off, inserting its own commentary, and has asked telephone callers to "role play" characters and hold fictitious conversations with each other on the phone-in line.

Music accounts for 50 per cent of programme time, a lot of it broadcast at night. A further ten hours, on average, is devoted to news and features and the rest is advertizing. Says Frederico Pedrocchi: "We keep advertizing down to five short spots an hour. To exceed this limit would change our whole concept of radio."

Where news and features are concerned there has always been a built-in dilemma for the Radio Popolare team. It would be a contradiction in terms, they concluded at the start, if their venture into socialist communication were to involve the same degree of selection and interpretation as that practised by the media "professionals". This contributed to the very process of stereotyping and distortion they were determined to avoid. Yet how were they to ensure a good standard of crisp, clearly presented material, attractive to a popular audience, without falling into the trap of speaking for people all the time?

The answer they arrived at, says Michele Cocuzza, was "to help people with the *way* they say things not with *what* they say". He explains how the radio decided to actively develop an alternative information network by inviting local people to act as correspondents in the schools, factories and neighbourhoods. Still others were asked to serve as resource people because of their experience in a particular field such as legal rights or trade unionism.

All these "collaborators" work closely with the radio's reporters, often speaking on programmes themselves and getting others from their communities or work places to do so. They take part in a weekly planning meeting of everyone involved in the radio, sessions which frequently extend into late night debates about the significance of this or that dispute at home or an overseas crisis like the martial law clampdown in Poland. Everyone has her/his ideas and sympathies with various tendencies on the left. But, says Frederico Pedrocchi, "we are non-sectarian and a fairly homogeneous group after six years."

In its news policy the radio neither adopts the "even-handed" philosophy of mainstream journalism nor thinks it has to push a collective view of its own on every question of the day. But the team's politics inform its approach and, using its correspondents' information and contacts as well as information from conventional channels such as news agencies, it tries to approach issues from the *perspective* of people suffering hardship and discrimination.

With international coverage as well, the news department tries to locate correspondents on the spot committed to the radio's objectives and to fighting oppression within their own countries. Priority is given to reporting from parts of the world where conflicts are taking place which, as the radio sees it, have particular implications for working people everywhere, e.g. Central America, Iran and Northern Ireland.

Women involved in the radio consider it their business to make sure that the perspective of women as the oppressed half of society comes across in the whole range of programmes. Twenty-five-year old Marina Terragni explained how, while many programmes broadcast have a special relevance to the problems of women, the radio had decided to drop its women's slot because "we didn't want to be in a ghetto". So now the woman in charge of international news, for example, brought her perspective to that coverage, as with a recent focus on women in El Salvador. Or the woman working on trade union related programmes, if talking about redundancy over the air, would point out its particular effects on women.

Marina Terragni thought that there should be more than the present 50 per cent of women working in the radio. Otherwise, she argued, it was easier for women's needs to get lost sight of. This had tended to happen in the station at a practical level where women were "doing more in advertizing and administration and less political work than the men".

The way that Radio Popolare has provided for disabled people to make their input is an illustration of how its participation-through-collaborators works. The full-time core group asked Giovanni Caloria, a well-known activist in the neighbourhood who has been blind from birth, to become a resource person. Giovanni runs a cooperative producing books and poetry on cassette for the blind and has written and campaigned widely on disablement as well as on other issues. The radio, he said, had encourged him without dictating what his input should be.

"The radio gives us (disabled people) a chance we wouldn't otherwise have," he went on. The disabled were fighting against being treated as objects of charity and kept in a separate compartment from the rest of society. It had therefore been agreed that he should contribute his insights and experience to many categories of programmes, not only those about disablement as such. On a programme discussing people's personal problems, for example, he had suggested bringing in a blind psychoanalyst to answer questions. On a programme dealing with legal rights he had inserted a section on the rights of the disabled.

Giovanni Caloria had brought housewives, factory workers and students from schools into the studio, among others. "I want to denounce the oppression of all who are marginalized and put the situation of disabled people in that context." This way, he argued, the marginalized could begin to combat a capitalist system which breeds injustice.

Signs of Radio Popolare's credibility with, and impact on, its chosen audience emerge in all sorts of circumstances. "People phone us if they see a burglary or an accident," smiles Michele Cocuzza. The radio's reporters have been allowed into meetings which have barred the media in general. The station has linked factories in their opposition to companies' authority measures. It is the only media space available to people from Milan's 30,000 strong Arab community whose members present a regular information programme in their own language. It has broadened public support for numerous campaigns such as those to stop prison torture and compulsory military service.

Having won a mass audience which identifies the station as "its" radio makes a vital difference to Radio Popolare's ability to find the funds to keep going. Out of a 1981 budget of 165 million lire, advertisements yielded 90 million. The rest came from those members of the public who supported the radio's fund-raising concerts or festivals or who bought Radio Popolare club cards entitling them to a small discount in certain shops and cinemas. All in all, the station's finances remain in a precarious state ("we really need 350 million lire to stay out of trouble"). Nevertheless, there's an underlying confidence that, as long as the station can go on providing a service that people value, the money will always turn up somehow.

Radio Popolare doesn't pretend to have completely solved the problem of professionalism, nor to have found a blueprint for socialist communication. But by helping people to communicate on a mass level across divisions of sex, age, educational background and party loyalties, and by emphasizing their common desire for fundamental change, the radio believes it can help to bring that day of change a little bit nearer.

### Protestant churches break out of their ghetto

Among the minority groups which have found a voice through the free radios are the Protestant churches in Italy. And they have wrestled with some tough theological questions in the process.

At one stage, in 1980, teams from Protestant congregations all over the country were participating in between 80 and 100 stations. Mainly Waldensians, Baptists, Methodists and Lutherans whose churches belong to the Italian Protestant Federation in Rome, they saw the phenomenon of independent radio as "an exceptional opportunity for the very small Italian Protestant minority to break out of its sociological and cultural ghetto".

The opportunity had been long in coming. Historically a persecuted minority in a country where Christian means Catholic and where the Catholic Church wields immense influence in every sphere of life, Protestants constitute less than one per cent of the 57 million population. Despite enjoying religious freedom nowadays they remain, as the statute books put it, an "authorized cult", kept strictly in their own compartment. Not surprisingly, the mass media have mostly ignored them.

One important job of the Italian Protestant Federation (FPI) when it was set up in 1967 to represent denominations 50,000 strong, was to help to raise the public profile of Protestantism in Italian society. The FPI press, radio and TV service, after an uphill battle, managed to make some inroads. Nevertheless, the impact of Protestant programmes on public radio and television channels has remained marginal compared to that of the Catholic Church. Through the Christian Democratic Party the Catholic establishment continued to make its presence felt in state broadcasting. And the Vatican runs its own network of shortwave radio stations.

The arrival of free radio not only broke the state monopoly of broadcasting. It also offered members of the Protestant community the chance, as they saw it, to dent the monopoly of the Catholic Church as the Christian reference point in Italy on all theological and social issues.

Evangelical churches such as the Assemblies of God, the Adventists and the Plymouth Brethren responded to free radio by buying their own stations. These three together owned 43 radios in 1980, many of them with a 24-hour output of preaching and gospel singing. Since the evangelical groups' funds are often topped up by wealthy parent churches in the US and elsewhere some of them can afford to buy time on commercial stations too.

Although the FPI maintains an open conversation with them it strongly disagrees with their approach to radio. Says FPI television and radio advisor, Renato Maiocchi: "We (Protestants) have a chance to be heard only if we come out of the ghetto."

Within its possibilities as a small coordinating body, the FPI endeavours to steer its churches away from acquiring their own stations and from preaching through the radio. It isn't easy. FPI director Giorgio Girardet, who also lectures in communication at the Protestant theological faculty in Rome, explains: "People think it's enough just to participate. They think the word of God is sufficient to push in itself."

Giorgio Girardet argues that the most appropriate place for Protestants to be heard is on the socialist stations or on stations run by opposition political parties like the Communist Party and Radical Party. They were usually the most willing to provide space for dissenting and oppressed groups. But more to the point, they helped to bring together people who feel the need to change society. "It matters to us what kind of programmes the radios (we use) broadcast," Giorgio Girardet insists. "It's naive to believe that it's possible to have an alternative voice in the wrong place."

In practice, Protestant groups have tended to snap up radio space where they could. Often this has meant broadcasting on socialist stations, but also on some commercial radios and, according to an FPI survey in 1980, on a few radios with extreme right wing leanings.

Protestant teams have mounted their own regular programmes, contributed views in round table discussions and even joined in the running of some stations. The fact remains, however, that many of their radio experiments which began with high hopes in the late 70s have either fizzled out completely or are just about ticking over.

Giorgio Girardet's overall assessment is a sober one. "They (Protestant programmes) have had no great results on our congregations or on the population," he says. For him this is not so much because of ownership change-overs among the free radios, though this is obviously disruptive for all those participating in them. Nor is it primarily a shortcoming of the radios. Rather, FPI soundings indicate several serious problems with the groups themselves.

Generally speaking these teams are tiny and under-resourced. Their commitment and interest is not always shared by their congregations as a whole. They have found it hard to sustain the necessary drive and to achieve a basic professional standard. They are from more affluent backgrounds than many of the people they want to reach and have trouble communicating in popular terms. They advocate social responsibility but not always from a basis of direct involvement on their part. And they are inclined to be more preoccupied with what they are saying than with who is listening.

The most enduring radio experiences of Protestant groups tend to take place in small rural towns such as those of the poorer south of Italy where the stations are fewer, where local needs show themselves clearly and where church members as individuals are already respected activists working to improve the community.

By contrast, in the industrial heartland of the north, local issues are also national, political life is intense and complex and dozens of radios jockey for space on the crowded wavebands. It is here that questions of which stations to participate in, on what terms and to what end, come up most sharply of all.

One Protestant group using radio in Milan, Italy's northern capital, turned Antonio di Pierro's living room into its recording studio. Antonio, a printer, lives with his family in a typical working class apartment complex a few blocks away from Radio Popolare. With tape recorders and papers strewn across carpet and sofa, he and four friends would regularly put together items for their programme on Radio Milano Libera, one of Milan's 120 independent radios.

The group members, Waldensians, Methodists and Baptists, dipped into their own pockets to buy their 5.6 million lire worth of equipment. All of them men with some previous interest in, or knowledge of radio, they wanted to reach a high professional standard in their venture.

Independent radio, they are convinced, represents "the most modern form of giving service to the community" and thus a new way of evangelizing. They chose Radio Milano Libera because it was a socialist station ("we would never have gone to a right-wing radio") and because it gave them an autonomous spot free of charge. From 1976-80, under the auspices of the Evangelical Federation of Lombardy, they presented their hour-long weekly programme.

As a rule, the group did not become involved in the life of the station other than discussing their input with the radio workers. This input was based on the assumption that Italians are largely ignorant of Protestantism and of the Bible. The team opted for a mixture of religious news, music, a history of Protestantism series and Bible meditations set in a daily life context, all pre-recorded. To these they added live studio discussions on new books, films or current events, raising all kinds of political and social issues — educational reform, violence, divorce, abortion, and so on.

For them this approach demonstrated that the practice of handing down moral dictates on this or that problem was not the only type of

Christianity on offer. It also constituted an effort of counter-information *per se*.

Each programme took three days to prepare — a heavy workload for five people holding down full-time jobs. Ernesto Ghizzoni, in his early twenties, the youngest of the group, voices disappointment that "not enough people in our churches were interested in helping". Neither was such a short programme each week enough to cultivate a regular audience, they concluded.

The group didn't know how many people listened to Radio Milano Libera. Reactions to their own programme took the form of an occasional letter or phone-in. (One listener asked them to stop talking and play more music!) They didn't convert people, they said, nor did they expect to. "The experience was more useful to us than to anyone else."

The fact of having to get away from clerical language had taught them a lot. But they hadn't overcome their lack of expertise to their own satisfaction. "If you present a broadcast in an interesting way you will be heard. If you present interesting subjects boringly it won't work. That's why professionalism's important."

Their regular programme came to a halt in 1980 when Radio Milano Libera ran short of cash, changed hands and reopened as Radio Città with a fresh programming policy. Since then Protestant participation in the station has been restricted to joining in occasional panel discussions. The change didn't take the group particularly by surprise. It even provided a respite for the five who were beginning to wilt under the pressure. Though they are still looking out for openings on other radios they believe that the only chance of the Protestant churches in their region making a lasting impact would be for the Evangelical Federation of Lombardy to launch its own radio. "Then we could give others the chance to speak and not the other way round."

In Turin, Italy's other major industrial centre of the north, Baptist and Waldensian churches have spent almost 6¼ million lire to put programmes on a commercial radio station. The city, sometimes called the fiefdom of Agnelli after the Fiat boss whose giant car plants dominate the industrial landscape, is served by some 70 free radios.

Since November 1981 the two Protestant denominations have been broadcasting on Radio Monte Bianco. This medium-power station, carrying a fairly fixed menu of music, soap opera and advertizing, places itself seventh in the audience ratings, with 36,000 regular and 265,000 occasional listeners out of a possible 600,000. The churches invested a total of 2¼ million lire in equipment plus two million lire each to buy a couple of half-hour programme slots every day for three years.

Volunteer groups from four local congregations, an average of eight people per group, take it in turns to make the programmes which they pre-record on cassettes several weeks in advance. In between meeting all together once a month to plan ahead, each group operates fairly autonomously. Pastors, office workers, students, teachers and technicians are involved, about the same number of women as men, and ranging in age from late teens to late forties.

The "recording centre" of one of the teams based in the Turin suburb of Rivoli is a converted language laboratory in a nearby Baptist college. Local Baptist pastor Franco Casanova, with two other members of the group, Patricia Femia and Adriano Giaiero, proudly show off their recording equipment and meticulously maintained tape library to visitors. "Through our programmes," they explain, "we have the chance to speak not only to those inside our churches but to others outside."

They had painstakingly taught themselves how to operate the equipment, and divided up among them the research work for different topics featured in the programmes. Like the Milan group they combined religious news, Bible meditations, music and discussions but emphasized as well questions of women's oppression and international issues like Poland and El Salvador.

A lot of politically committed people in Italy had left the Catholic Church because they saw it as a barrier to change, Franco Casanova pointed out. Many Protestant churches, on the other hand, were rooted in the socialist tradition and should demonstrate through radio the fact that "our Protestant line coincides with our political line".

Protestant broadcasts on Radio Monte Bianco go out morning and evening. The evening programme at 18.00 hours is always new while the morning one at 11.00 hours is a repeat of the previous day. Taking time on a commercial station, for Franco Casanova, is like having "a clear voice in a mess". The church had to live with the contradictions such a contract produced. "We are against the consumer society but we are using a tool of the consumer society," he said.

Adriano Giaiero, for his part, sees commercial radio as the best option. On socialist stations, he argued, Protestants were often used to express a general religious viewpoint and were not understood as Protestant. Alternatively, if you paid for your own space on a commercial radio you could stress your separate identity, evangelize in your own way, and reach a wider audience into the bargain. What the audience figures were for Radio Monte Bianco they did not know and feedback from their programmes was confined to a few phone calls and letters.

For the future they favour having a station owned by their churches, not as an exclusive loudspeaker for them but as a radio "which gathers together all Protestant and Catholic voices". Such a project was currently under consideration. "But the airwaves are so crowded we are waiting for a radio to die."

---

• The writer wishes to thank Prof. John Downing of the Communications Department, Hunter College, The City University of New York, for his assistance with the research on Radio Popolare for this chapter. John Downing is the author of *The Media Machine* (Pluto Press, London, UK, 1980) and *The Politics of Alternative Media* (South End Press, Boston, MA 02116, USA, 1983).

# Rural movements find a voice

Under the proud eye of parents and neighbours a dozen village youngsters are putting on a play. It's a common enough sight in the Western Caribbean where people will act out a story as soon as tell it.

In this case, although most of the performers are children, there is nothing childish about their theme. A "landowner" is evicting a "tenant farmer" because he has found a more profitable use for the land. When the peasant protests, a "policeman" arrives, toy gun in hand, to escort the troublesome farmer to court and is slipped some money by the landowner for this timely intervention. Several scenes later young fists are raised in the air in a rousing finale: "We should struggle against those who take our land."

This is the village of Estero in the Dominican Republic, the small sugar-growing country which shares the Caribbean island of Hispaniola with Haiti. The children of Estero learn early on what kind of problems await them. All 500 people in their village depend for their survival on small-holdings totalling less than one acre. The state uses nearly all the rest of the arable land available for sugar cane plantations.

Like many villages in the south-west, Estero is very cut off. There is no telephone, newspapers are a rarity and public transport, apart for the odd donkey, is non-existent. Yet the farmers and their families are well aware that peasant communities miles away are suffering the same problems. They have formed their own local branch of the peasants' confederation and, as the children's play suggests, are learning not to take injustice lying down.

This is due, in no small measure, to the radio. Said one old man: "The first and only school we have is Radio Enriquillo." Radio staff trained the young village woman who produced the children's drama. The radio brought them news of a massive land invasion by peasants further north. The radio waged a campaign against the authorities until the main bridge for the region, destroyed by a hurricane, was rebuilt. It is the radio which broadcasts calls for assistance when the village irrigation pump breaks down and messages from families to their relatives in cases of emergency.

Radio Enriquillo's small broadcasting station is in the market town of Tamayo, a couple of hours' drive from Estero along a rough road through the sugar plantations. Its ten kilowatt transmitter standing high above the green, blue and purple wood houses makes it easy to spot. And should a first-time visitor be in any doubt, the noble head of "Enriquillo", an Indian leader who fought the Spanish conquerors, is painted on the outside wall.

The low, yellow building, once a convent, now houses a broadcasting studio, interview corner, tape library, offices and meeting rooms. Local people mill around in the reception space as music going out over the air is relayed via a loudspeaker. The announcer for the next shift arrives on his donkey. Villagers hand over crumpled notes with messages and news items.

In Latin America where poorer sections of the community must have their own alternative communications outlets if they are to achieve any independent organization or voice, the phenomenon of local public-service radios has become well known.

Many of these radios are church-supported and are trying to act as allies of the oppressed. But few set a greater store by involving the people they aim to serve than Radio Enriquillo. Its trademark is a string of *buzones* (mail boxes) in all the towns and villages of the region in which listeners place their local news, letters, answers to quizzes and invitations to the radio team to visit their communities. Its recording studio can be the market place, the slumhouse or the meeting room. Its philosophy is summed up by a poster on the office wall: "Communication is giving a voice to the voiceless."

The radio was the idea of two Belgian Catholic priests, Humberto Vandenbulcke and Andrés Geerts, plus Cuban writer José Ignacio

López Vigil who used to work for a radio school, Radio Santa Maria. They set up the station in Tamayo in 1977 with funds from a church agency in Holland. Their work in the parishes and contact with all kinds of grassroots organizations convinced them that a radio could play a valuable role in putting groups in touch with each other, in strengthening the community by giving expression to its rich folk culture and, ultimately, in providing a mouthpiece for an independent peasant movement in-the-making.

Others came along who shared this commitment to the people of the countryside. Among them was social worker Felicia Fermin from Santiago and Argelia Estevez, a physicist who used to teach at the university in the capital, Santo Domingo. "We thought when we came", remembers Felicia, "that we would have to provide an alternative (medium) and we found it ready-made." Argelia never regretted leaving the city. "It is more interesting when you are telling and building the story of a people," she says.

These five staff now form the nucleus of a bigger team of 22 workers and the station is owned by a cooperative foundation of 24 lay people, priests, sisters and the bishop of Barahona diocese, Favio Rivas.

The radio operates in a country where thirty years of dictatorship has left a legacy of fear and underdevelopment. A former Spanish colony with 5.5 million people, the Dominican Republic lived under brutal dictator Trujillo until 1961. Any chance of fundamental social reforms afterwards was nipped in the bud when 40,000 US marines crushed the left wing Bosch regime in 1965. The United States continues to dominate the country's political and economic life.

While industry has been boosted in the towns, thinly-populated sugar-growing areas such as the south-west, where Tamayo is situated, have remained neglected and are particularly punished by the country's current economic crisis.

Peasant organizations were ruthlessly repressed by successive governments. Until a few years ago, a radio like Radio Enriquillo, attempting to give them a voice, would have been closed down overnight. For the time being there is a limited space under the ruling Dominican Revolutionary Party (PRD), though no-one knows how long it will last.

Of the 131 radio stations in the Dominican Republic, two are operated by the government and five, including Radio Enriquillo, by religious foundations. The rest are commercial stations broadcasting mainly Americanized music, the occasional news flash and lots of advertizing.

The founders of Radio Enriquillo knew from the start what they *didn't* want their station to be. "There is no place here for vertical communication pushing fixed formulas to a passive, anonymous audience." Neither would it be the kind of Christian station that used the radio as a pulpit. Direct evangelization efforts by Catholic missionaries had, in any case, made very little impact on the people whose popular religiosity involves an odd mixture of Christian concepts and Dominican voodoo and who have no sense of belonging to a church.

Many priests and sisters had opted to evangelize indirectly by living alongside the farmers, workers and slum-dwellers, sharing their poverty. In the same way, said the radio team, they would start from the real world and real problems of the peasants. The main difference would be that, as a mass medium, their radio would seek to work at a mass level with the clear objective of raising consciousness and cementing the struggles of those who were trying to change their situation.

From 5 in the morning until 11 at night every day the radio can be picked up by all those within an 80-kilometre radius of Tamayo — some half a million people. It presents a lively round of home-grown music, poetry and drama, news, discussion programmes, religious meditations and programmes for children and teenagers.

Collaborating closely with parish workers and animators from other voluntary organizations, the radio producers spend a lot of time in the community interviewing listeners, identifying the issues that concern them most and evaluating previous programmes with them. Once regular contact has been established, each community appoints its correspondent to channel information to the radio. Local farmers groups — there are 200 in the region — and women's organizations also send in news of their activities. And youth and children exchange letters, problems, favourite stories, music requests and birthday dedications through their own Enriquillo listeners' clubs.

All this wasn't achieved overnight. "At first people were surprised and amused to be consulted for their opinions," explained Juan Tomás Olivero who carried out some of that early groundwork. But once they had heard themselves on radio, he added, they became very enthusiastic. The first time one Tamayo woman heard her neighbour expressing an opinion on the air she rushed around to the person's house to continue the discussion!

From the moment the people began to feel at home with the radio, even those who could hardly read and write, and began to articulate their needs, there has been no shortage of broadcasting material. The biggest scandal in the area is the slave-like conditions of the Haitian sugar plantation workers who migrate across the nearby border desperate for a job. The men toil from dawn till dusk to earn just $1.80 for every ton of cane they cut, and live with their families in squalid *bateys* (barracks) separated from the towns.

Lack of land, credit provision and access to the irrigation channels kept for sugar, are the farmers' main grievances. Women feel the injustice of being paid less than men if they pick crops on the big estates, and of carrying the main burden of keeping their families going on pitifully low incomes. The youth (50 per cent of the population around Tamayo) rarely get anything beyond the most basic education, then travel miles in search of work, and all in a society where there is an almost total absence of leisure facilities or meeting places for them.

All these issues and many more have been talked out among communities via the radio. In the "Encounter" programme, for example, a particular problem is dramatized or discussed at the beginning of the week. Next, cassettes of the programme are taken to the villages by animators who record the people's reactions. Finally, an edited version of the programme is re-broadcast over the latter days of the week, gradually incorporating more and more comments and letters from listeners and discussing what action can be taken.

As well as cassettes for community groups the radio also produces lively comics with cartoon drawings done by one of the young announcers. Some booklets, easily understood by people who can't read, echo the themes of the programmes and can be used while listening or separately. Others offer humorous hints and information about how to make local associations and village meetings better organized and more democratic.

The latest comic series, by José Ignacio López Vigil, is a Latin American version of "Animal Farm" *(Granja Latina),* the famous allegory of the degeneration of the Russian revolution. Regular episodes of José Ignacio's controversial radio soap opera *Un Tal Jesús* ("A Certain Jesus") about Jesus' life, were run by Radio Enriquillo backed up by discussion guides. The series, which depicts Jesus as a simple man who denounces the injustices done to the poor, contains obvious parallels with Latin America today. It won a popular following in the Dominican Republic and in other countries until it was deemed dangerous and disrespectful by the Latin American Conference of Bishops which banned its use.

In the lead-up to the 1982 general elections, Radio Enriquillo produced a series of programmes, plus a special booklet, explaining what the elections were about. Animators interviewed villagers to gather their reactions to the local campaigns of the various candidates. Then news writer and presenter Ramón Urbaez interviewed each candidate on the air.

News has a key place in the programme schedule and overall philosophy of Radio Enriquillo. Says Ramón: "We try to convey that the world isn't an incomprehensible thing. It can be managed and problems can be solved."

When 27 year-old Ramón, a self-taught journalist, first joined the radio from his home in the capital, director Humberto Vandenbulcke put a photo of an elderly peasant couple beside his typewriter "to remind me who I was writing for". And if he still needed bringing down to earth, a spell of working on "Encounter" made sure of that. "The misery and despair I saw in the villages made a big impression on me."

The Enriquillo news office, responsible for two half-hour slots daily plus a longer magazine programme on Saturdays, must be one of the few of its kind to operate without a telephone (Tamayo has no phone links) or a telex machine. It relies instead on the main daily papers, read very critically, and above all, on a powerful short-wave radio. The radio picks up news from agencies and other radios all over Central and Latin America — everything from "Voice of America" to the radio of El Salvador's guerrilla fighters.

The staff think that the news coverage by commercial radios and the national press is disjointed, sensationalized and "pushes the interests of the ruling class". Also, they point out, the commercial media tend to regard the south-west, with only six per cent of the country's population, as insignificant and pay little attention to events there.

Radio Enriquillo uses its network of village correspondents to get a broad view of what is happening in the region. It divides programmes into regional, national and international segments. It employs simple language, adds background information to put subjects in context, and never mentions a country without explaining where it is and summarizing the general situation there.

Listeners who can barely read and have never travelled far outside their area are able to differentiate between US President Reagan and former President Carter. They know what happened to the Solidarity movement in Poland. Martyred Archbishop Romero of El Salvador is now a household name among them.

When different sources put different interpretations on events the programme will report: "The Voice of America says... and Radio Havana says..." If a row blows up about the business practices of a transnational corporation the radio quotes both the grievances of the community affected and the benefits which the company claims to have brought to the country. "We let people draw their own conclusions."

Ramón explains how the radio team, anxious to acquire the necessary technical skills to build up a good news service, had started off by employing professional journalists. This approach, however, had backfired. The journalists regarded their work for the radio as just another job. Their conventional training proved, if anything, a disadvantage. Sensationalism interested them more than information that would benefit the area. Most of all, says Ramón, "they had a built-in perspective of the ruling class and their words and concepts were not those of the people".

The present writers believe that they have refined their approach as they have become more involved in the region. This doesn't mean they feel they can dispense with professional competence. They have all in the past acted as correspondents for newspapers while doing other jobs. But they regard a commitment to the people, and an understanding of the conditions under which they live, as their prime qualification. Their yardstick nowadays is always "to look at news in the same way as the poor would look at it and ask what would be useful to them".

Cooperation works well between Radio Enriquillo and *El Nuevo Diario,* a new daily paper whose editor, Juan Bolivar Diaz, fled the repression in the 70s following an attempt on his life. "The factor that unites the radio and ourselves", said Diaz during a visit to the station, "is a concept of service to the people. And in collaboration with the radio we can give national coverage to issues (of the southwest) which wouldn't be widely known."

Church workers greeted the arrival of Radio Enriquillo with mixed feelings originally. Those clergy who believe that the better-off can be pressed to help the poor saw (and still see) the radio's philosophy as too partisan. It could better use its resources, they insist, for more religious programming, thereby raising the traditionally weak public profile of the church in their region. Other priests and nuns who opted to show solidarity with the poor by sharing their hardships doubted whether a powerful mass medium imposed "from outside" could promote this process.

For the majority of the latter, even if some tensions still remain, the radio has now proved itself many times over. Says the parish

priest of Tamayo: "It's incredible how the radio has been able to in-
tegrate itself into the life of the people — to walk with the people. It
has become part of their lives like the sun rising."

Just how great a part was demonstrated by dramatic events in
1982. In February of that year 2,000 peasants in the San Juan area of
the north of Tamayo invaded privately owned land. Their tiny im-
poverished plots, they said, could no longer support them and their
families. Radio Enriquillo brought news of the invasion, reported
that police had arrested 1,500 and relayed appeals to other communities for protest action. Within hours the peasant associations of
the south-west had occupied local authority offices, held vigils in the
churches, organized a demonstration and sent food and money to
those in jail.

Official promises that more land would be made available were not
kept and the struggle goes on. Meanwhile graffiti covering walls
along the Tamayo road proclaim: "Land and liberty to the
peasants!"

The plight of the 40,000 Haitians in the area is a political hot
potato and the government stopped the radio broadcasting programmes for these workers in their own Creole language. Other regular
programmes, however, with information received from Haitian
"correspondents", have continued to highlight the needs of the
destitute plantation communities. They have taken a strong stand, in
the process, against racial attitudes of Dominican workers towards
Haitians, arguing that such prejudices only play into the hands of
those who would exploit them all.

The radio covered the first-ever strike by the Haitians who complained that the plantations' scales for weighing the cane had been
fixed in order to cheat them out of the money due to them. Further
protests in 1982 about unpaid bonuses led to the harassment of
several of their leaders. The radio, together with the Guild of Journalists, led a campaign for the release of one of its Haitian correspondents arrested on a trumped-up subversion charge. On being
freed, the man made a statement on the air about how he had been
tortured in jail.

Women's groups throughout the south-west provinces have also
come to see Radio Enriquillo as "their" radio. The first women's
programmes included "standard" ingredients like entertainment and
cooking recipes. "We were well aware that, with the recipes, we were
reinforcing the traditional view of women's role," admits Felicia Fermin, "but listeners requested them." The programmes' producers,
she explained, saw them as one device for attracting an audience

and gradually steering it towards other topics such as health and nutrition.

Yet even when they began to touch on these questions too, the producers and their collaborators from the women's association in the region sometimes found themselves at odds with reality. They would give women advice about the nutrition value of milk and meat only to discover that many couldn't afford either. They could stress the importance of vaccinations only to find that some villagers had no medical facilities of any kind. Says Luisa Féliz of the women's association, Promoción del Mujer del Sur: "We decided that, if we just broadcast without having contact with the grassroots, our programmes weren't worth anything."

From then on, the women's association workers and radio animators made a concerted effort to interview the women in the villages and began encouraging them to form their own groups. Today there are some 2,000 members, many of whom are in frequent contact with the radio, sending in their requests and points of view. "These are women", says Luisa, "who are now organized collectively and who are prepared to get out of the house and make demands." They had led community campaigns for clean water, street lights and health care and were very aware of their own rights as women.

As women's consciousness has developed so have their demands to the radio about the problems they want to see tackled. The women's association now has its own 20-minute slot every week and other programmes have broached issues such as equal pay, domestic violence and sexual stereotypes. In 1982 the Tamayo area held its first ever International Women's Day celebrations which the radio covered.

The presence of women on the radio staff, who also have their own study group, has helped to ensure that the station's support for women in the region has remained consistent, Felicia believes. "Men used to write to the radio and say, 'You're turning our women into tigers'," she laughs. "We have tried to show that women's liberation is also men's liberation from male chauvinism and aim to unite women and men to confront their common problems like low wages."

Strong endorsement for the radio's principle of serving the people, Christians as well as others, comes from the Bishop of Barahona diocese, Fabio Rivas, who sits on the board of management. However, he thinks that the radio team's "style of work" is bringing the church under a lot of unnecessary scrutiny and pressure. "If you (work) from a Christian evangelical point of view you'll be respected," he says. "But if the (work) of Christians is done in a political style which involved taking sides then (they) will be persecuted because of groups they associate or don't associate with."

Three religious recently deported had made that mistake, the Bishop said. He was therefore unable to intervene successfully on their behalf. He had been obliged to defend Radio Enriquillo in the face of non-believers in the power structures who were unhappy about its leftist language and methodology — as were some clergy. "Up to now we have helped (the radio team) because we consider them a church organization. If ever they decide that they are not we'll have to think again."

Local groups see Radio Enriquillo as a church radio, argues Gerrard Rogmans of Equippo Lemba, an organization of educator-animators working with farmers in the area for the last ten years. "If it wasn't a church organization it wouldn't survive and the people know that too. They see it as priests doing it. They see that it's totally different from other radio stations and who else but the church would run something like that?"

"It's because of the church and Radio Enriquillo that we have a little freedom — our only freedom," says a Haitian leader as he sits surrounded by his children in his cramped, bare hut. "Before the radio came we were in the dark — it has brought light into our lives. Since we have found our voice through the radio we've become stronger and we will never go back to what we were."

For radio staff members like Andrés Geerts who was there from the start, the station is one *means* towards creating new kind of society, not an *end* in itself. And it is just as much a ministry as having a parish. "Gospel values", says Andrés simply, "are the values from which we drink."

By no means are the people of Enriquillo completely satisfied with themselves. On the financial side, because money in the Catholic Church in the Dominican Republic has always been in short supply, they have been forced to look outside the country for over half the station's $120,000 annual budget. And the bulk of that contribution still comes from the Dutch church agency which helped them from the beginning.

Advertizing (a maximum of 40 minutes of airtime a day for specified basic products is accepted) raises $20,000 a year, though there is scant prospect of increasing that source of income as long as the buying-power of the region remains so low. Meanwhile, the launch of an overdue training programme and keeping up with high inflation has pushed up funds needed for 1983 by an extra $60,000.

There is still room for improvement, too, in combining the work of the radio with that of the priests and sisters working at the grassroots. This would also feed into the religious programming. Up to now, apart from *Un Tal Jesús,* religious broadcasts have tended to follow a familiar formula of meditations, prayers and a Sunday morning worship, and have been the least participatory of any of the radio's programmes.

Looking to the future, Andrés Geerts believes that until the radio becomes truly a medium *of* the people in the sense of rural movements running the station and producing their own programmes, there is always a risk of the original philosophy going off course. "As long as we are the ones who take the decisions it's dangerous," he says.

Conscious of this, the staff are going to no small lengths, through training and consultation, to prepare for the day when they hope to hand over the reins. Over 1983-1986, a fifth of the total budget will be devoted to providing a training course for the radio's pool of fifty unpaid collaborators and group leaders, that is, over and above the informal instruction in recording and scripting that they already receive.

Consultation comes first when any new comic book series is produced. Soundings are taken from the communities and from the animators of the popular education groups working with them, and drafts are thrashed out until a final version is agreed upon.

The biggest consultation exercise to date came in 1981 when a survey was carried out over three months to solicit the opinions of local people, pastoral agents and animators about the usefulness of the radio for their concerns and work. Town meetings and workshops were held beforehand to determine what questions should be asked in the survey. The investigation itself involved 120 personal interviews, 30 meetings and the distribution of 1,400 questionnaires.

When the results are finally processed they will be written up and re-submitted to all the people who took part in meetings for their approval before being published. Findings of the survey indicate, in the main, a hearty vote of confidence in the radio and they furnish a rich fund of information on which the radio can now build its future work.

Accountability is stressed as much in the internal running of the station as in its dealings with the community. Staff are responsible to the 24-member board and its executive committee. The board, in turn, reports to a yearly assembly open to representatives of local associations, of congregations, of religious orders and anyone else committed to the project who can buy a 200 peso ($200) share and become a member. The staff elect their own representatives for the board and assembly, too, and say that they have a strong voice in both.

If Radio Enriquillo had opted to become a religious station or a radio school it would undoubtedly be a lot more politically and financially secure than it is today. Instead, it has chosen the long and risky road of working for social change in a way which is, by definition, very exposed. The people's movements in the rural areas of the Dominican Republic lack the experience and political cohesion of the workers' movement in the cities. Peasants of the south-west are not yet strong enough to protect the radio, and the church may not be prepared to for much longer. Nevertheless, for those who work for the station and the many who support it the radio is only one stepping stone towards the kind of society they want to build. They have come far enough to know that even if the worst happens and the radio is silenced, the faith and vision behind it will survive.

# Fighting apartheid
# from the grassroots

The residents of Mitchell's Plain were after the city council's blood. Their suburb, a new housing area 20 kilometres from the centre of Cape Town, South Africa, was supposed to be a showpiece development for "Coloured" (mixed race) people. But its 100,000 inhabitants faced the same basic problem as those in other townships. Wages were so low that they couldn't afford the essentials of life. What was the point, they asked, of having maisonettes with the "luxury" of electricity if many families were forced to leave their lights switched off because they lacked the money to pay the bill?

Everyone's electricity bill fell due the third week of the month — before the majority of workers received their next wages. And if they were late they had to pay extra as a penalty so they just slipped further into arrears. What would be an inconvenience in some contexts was a source of real suffering in this one.

The Electricity Petition Committee, formed by some residents to get the due date of the electricity bills changed, conducted a random survey of 400 families in Mitchell's Plain. They discovered that seven out of every ten households paid their electricity accounts late. A quick piece of arithmetic indicated that, taking the community as a whole, the Council was cashing in on their poverty to the tune of R400,000* a year in penalty money.

Determined, then, to organize a mass campaign, the Electricity Petition Committee shared its findings with their local paper, *Grassroots Community Newsletter*. No reporter was sent to interview them. Instead, half a dozen members of the committee sat down as part of a small news group at the paper. Together they worked out a story explaining why a campaign was needed, why people should get involved, and how a public meeting was being held at Lentaguer Civic Centre. They also devised a heading and cartoon for the article and decided to give it front-page treatment.

The finalized text and layout were taken back to the full committee for its approval. Then the story was in print — "The Big Lights Rip-Off" — illustrated with a city council bulb full of cash.

The Sunday morning after *Grassroots* came out, Mitchell's Plain volunteers gathered as usual to sell the paper door-to-door. They had been briefed beforehand about the electricity issue so that they could draw people's attention to the story and invite them to the meeting. By late afternoon they finished their rounds and saturated the streets around the venue for the meeting with extra copies.

Three thousand people turned up for the meeting. Two days later they marched on the city council's offices bearing banners and petitions...

The next edition of *Grassroots* was able to report a victory for the electricity campaign, one which benefited everyone in Cape Town. Later on, in an end-of-year round up of recent happenings, the paper noted: "This year (1981), our struggles have been located in areas such as Mitchell's Plain, Bonteheuwel, Nyanga, Bishop Lavis and many others. While we need to continue to build strong democratic people's organizations, we also need to break this isolation and link our local struggles into mass struggles."

Increasingly in the land of apartheid black opposition is finding expression regionally through trade union battles and community mobilizations and tangible issues such as education, rents and, as in Mitchell's Plain, electricity.

Little of the real extent of these people's problems or their organizational efforts can be gleaned from the mass media. Instead "the black viewpoint" is mainly presented through those representing moderate or conservative black opinion. Ample coverage is

---

* One US dollar = Rand 1.06.

given, too, to compliant, racially separate management committees and councils created by the government.

In the Western Cape, as elsewhere in South Africa, the black population is catered for by low-grade soap operas and shows in the vernacular on government-controlled radio and TV. Commercial newspapers employing black journalists have introduced slick, glossy supplements to tap the market in the black areas. With their pin-ups, carnival and crime reports, these supplements project a predictably superficial and sensationalized view of township life. *Grassroots Community Newsletter,* however, sets out to do exactly the opposite.

No concern of the community brought to *Grassroots* goes unreported, whether it is a residents group's fight for more bus shelters or a massive campaign for union recognition at a factory. The paper has brought together 70 affiliated black organizations in the Western Cape — residents' associations, trade unions, youth and women's groups, social services organizations, teachers and students who write articles, distribute each issue or use *Grassroots* as a tool in their campaigns. And though the operation is local its goal is far broader. Argued a recent editorial: "It is only when we are organized on the factory floor and in the places where we live and when our organizations come together, that we will be truly strong to press forward in our struggle for a free and democratic South Africa."

*Grassroots'* bright red masthead first saw the light of day in January 1980. Since then it has appeared at roughly five-week intervals. The 16-page English language tabloid has increased its print-run from 5,000 at the start to 30,000 copies and won an estimated 200,000 readers throughout the Cape Peninsula, especially in the Cape Flats around Cape Town.

Its first base was a tiny office shared with the domestic workers' union office in the centre of old Cape Town. Now "home" is a bigger room nearby, partitioned into three, and symbolically located opposite the former headquarters of the city council, the paper's favourite target!

Two black journalists from Cape Town newspapers and a community worker launched *Grassroots* with the help of a grant from the black journalists' union, the Writers' Association of South Africa. They had been putting their heads together with local people who saw the need to publicize and coordinate some of the embryo community organizations emerging in the Western Cape at that time.

It was a particularly difficult moment to start a paper. Some political publications along with most black political organizations had been banned. But as a non-profit newsletter not subject to the registration requirements of monthly and weekly papers and spotlighting issues from a local and not overtly political standpoint, *Grassroots* found a legal space. Its originators had no models to follow; their project was the first of its kind in the country. Still, they were determined to make it a paper which would "articulate the news, views and aspirations of the oppressed and be their voice". *Grassroots'* "alternative" features start with the price, kept at a modest 15c to make it accessible. It also looks different. Partnering bold headlines and black and white pics are lots of drawings and cartoon strips explaining "The rise in bread prices", "Why we demand a hospital" or "What to do if your child gets worms". Adverts occupy less than a third of the space and are sales spots for local traders only.

The distribution is different. Most of the copies are sold door to door, at public events or at house meetings by volunteers who use it at the same time to mount membership drives for their organizations.

News and information receive different treatment. "It makes no sense", say contributors, "to report that the bread price has increased without saying *why* this is so. It makes no sense to write about low wages without linking it to the bosses' chase for profits or to demand that the local housing authority repair residents' houses without stating that this is necessary because our people do not have a political voice in local or central government."

Finally, *Grassroots* is different in the way it involves the community. Before the project even started more than 50 residents' and worker organizations were consulted, invited to serve on a central committee, to submit reports of their activities and assist with distribution. By March 1982 when the second annual general meeting was held, 150 representatives from local organizations and publications groups nationally attended.

The idea is that delegates from affiliated groups "must be able to see the same democratic process at work in *Grassroots* as in their own organizations". So they serve on the paper's general decision-making body assisted by an elected executive and four full-time staff members.

Many groups make a still more direct input at news-gathering and layout sessions. On average representatives from 15 groups plus interested individuals join in the news meetings where a list of stories for the next issue is drawn up, and decisions are taken about who will write what and, at the final stage, where drafts are read out and agreed on. Then on printing day a further 50 volunteers invade the small offset litho printshop in Athlone township and amidst chatter and laughter fold and collate all the copies.

Teams handling news and production have staff member Mike, an experienced journalist, to lend them a hand. The three other full-timers are Steve, dealing with advertizing and distribution, administrative assistant Marlene, and Leila, the permanent organizer who used to be a volunteer from the local social workers' group and who now has the task of coordinating the entire operation.

*Grassroots* has no leaders. Everyone involved feels strongly that the newsletter should present a collective face to the community. There are no by-lines on articles. The names of individuals rarely receive a mention in stories. Rather it is their organizations that are highlighted.

Stories presented in the paper are never simply "news". The news team explains: "We would ask how can this article contribute to initiating organization or strengthen it? Does it expose the injustices in our society? How can it best be written from the people's point of view at a level where it relates to their experiences? Will it inform and educate — raise a critical awareness among the oppressed?"

This approach gives *Grassroots* four main ingredients. Coverage of existing campaigns and achievements provides encouragement by example... a union-run workers' clinic opened in Paarl... villages near Caledon cutting food costs through bulk buying... four townships challenging rent increases... seed potato workers near Ceres forcing management to double their wages through strike action...

Exposés and reports of protest highlight the need for organizations to be formed... "20,000 object to fares increases"... "Tafelsig residents call for schools"... "Anger over Lotus River evictions" ...

Educative features on the centre pages discuss the strengths and weaknesses of different campaigns and explain wider issues like the Labour Relations Bill which could affect them...

An illustrated "Advice" section at the back promotes basic self-reliance by offering guidance on a multiplicity of day-to-day problems. A regular panel of community and social workers with experience in fields such as health, law, education and trade unions have charge of this section. They cover topics like "How to claim maternity pay", "Your rights when under arrest", "Your rights when laid off from work", "The danger of lung disease for textile workers", "Underweight children", "The benefits of breast-feeding"...

The hardest-hit sections of the community find a ready-made forum in the pages of *Grassroots*. During the schools' boycott several students and their parents were interviewed about the crisis to help cement understanding between the two groups. And youth movements with their meetings and cultural rallies now form the backbone of contributors and helpers.

Also covered extensively is the United Women's Organization (UWO), busy building its 32 branches in the Cape after a successful founding conference in April 1981. One woman quoted in a recent UWO article told how "high rents, bus fares, food prices, poor housing and lack of services such as crèches weigh heavily on our (women's) shoulders as we try to make ends meet". Another called on her sisters to come together to fight the labour preference system which imposes unskilled and badly-paid jobs like domestic service on African women and the pass laws which break up their families. "We cannot sit back and do nothing" she declared.

In its straightforward language, punchy style and lively overall format *Grassroots* clearly bears the imprint of professional journalists. In fact black journalists living in the townships lend a lot of weight to news gathering and production and share their skills with the other helpers.

They admit that in the initial stages very few stories were written by the local people themselves. "It's hard finding a balance between community participation and technical know-how." News writing, they felt, was a completely new experience for the people, many of whom did not have the confidence to put over their views. The technical production process took a long time to master as well. "But with experience and training things are improving."

*Grassroots* has run a good number of workshops to teach local group members the basics of writing, cartooning, layout and printing. The role of the newsletter as a medium, its limitations, distribution and feedback were included. One workshop helped the Bellville Youth Association to create its own news sheet. Another session incorporated advice for college students on how they could use newsletters or school magazines as teaching aids.

For *Grassroots* to achieve representative news coverage of the townships is no easy matter. Participation and distribution tend, by definition, to be stronger in the best organized localities and weakest where a self-help infrastructure is lacking. And even in areas of strongest support it is hard for the newsletter to keep the same trained helpers. The bigger their organizations become the more demands are made on them and the less time they have to devote to the paper as such.

Finances, though, are the biggest strain. All four staff receive the same minimal salaries. Their jobs require them to be skilled community workers, and they are continually overloaded, but funds are too tight to employ extra people. Printing and typesetting costs swallow up nearly half the total budget and have practically doubled since the paper started. "There have been times", staff say, "when salaries could not be paid or when the printer refused to print because he hadn't received his last cheque."

Ten issues of the paper were published in 1982 with a total budget of R70,000. Up to now, the paper has managed to generate 50 per cent of its money locally from sales, regular pledges from helpers and from advertizing, while outside sponsors supply the rest. Most of the other half comes from an outside church agency.

Through this lifeline and through local action in the parishes, the church has shown its wholehearted commitment to the battles being fought in the townships and strengthened by *Grassroots*. Congregations on the spot have signed petitions, opened their church doors to residents' meetings and collected money for striking workers. Christians and Muslims work side by side distributing *Grassroots* as part of community campaigns, even though Muslim-Christian divisions in Cape society sometimes run deep at institutional level.

The church agency backing *Grassroots* financially does so without requiring any Christian credentials from the project. "For us the value system reflected in the paper and its concept of service is what the gospel is all about." In so far as criteria come up, it is *Grassroots* which sets them. Its workers believe that in a community where the churches are one grouping among several, coverage of them in the paper should be according to what they contribute rather than who they are. This was explained during a recent evaluation meeting in answer to a question about why there was not more about the church and religion in the paper. *Grassroots,* came the reply, did not see its role as promoting religious organizations and denominations as such. And this could, in the Cape context, be divisive. "However, in as much as it is part of our life and struggles the church should certainly be there in the paper."

Advertizing, regarded as "a contradiction that we will have to live with", provides a lot of the locally-earned cash. Nevertheless, saturation point has been reached with publicity solicited from community tradespeople and more money could only be earned if advertizing from big retail businesses and multinational firms were accepted.

A recent annual general meeting, however, threw out this option and upheld existing policy, wary of *Grassroots* becoming dependent on big business to a point where it was compromised. If, the delegates pointed out, advertizing were accepted from Simba Chips and if a strike took place at the Simba Chips Plant which the paper supported, the paper would be placed in a tricky political situation.

Like many publications in South Africa, *Grassroots* has suffered state repression. Founder-member and first organizer Johnny Issel was forced out of his job after a year because of a banning order. Then in 1981 two editions of the newsletter and its calendar were banned, though the bannings on the papers were subsequently contested successfully under the Publications Appeal Procedure. A *Grassroots* editorial informed readers of the authorities' attempts to cripple the paper, assuring them that it had nonetheless come through as strong as ever. "We refuse to be silenced," the editorial declared.

Problems have indeed been plentiful up to now, yet so have rewards. In 1980 the paper won the Henry Nxumalo Award for its outstanding contribution to journalism in South Africa, given by the Media Workers' Association. The paper's development and its training workshops have helped to stimulate an avalanche of mimeographed news sheets and leaflets by local groups in the Western Cape and have provided a lead for the launch, in Pretoria, Johannesburg, Durban and Port Elizabeth, of other newsletters in the *Grassroots* vein.

*Grassroots* consistently publicized the 1980 schools' boycott, and received its "most significant endorsement" when students used it as discussion material in awareness classes they ran for themselves. Similarly, its coverage gave a local boost to the 1981 bus boycott in which hundreds of township residents walked miles to work in a successful protest to prevent steep fares increases by the bus companies.

The newsletter was also prominent in helping to build what is now the Cape's largest umbrella organization for black groups, the Cape Areas Housing Action Committee (CAHAC). Says the CAHAC steering committee: "*Grassroots* helps to promote the work of organizations affiliated to CAHAC and in so doing serves to strengthen (us). It takes us into the homes of many residents whom we constantly need to keep in touch with."

Growing reader loyalty to the paper and the issues it champions shows through in articles and letters. After *Grassroots* had helped to promote the sweets boycott called in 1981 in support of sacked Wilson Rowntree factory workers in the Eastern Cape, a 12 year-old girl wrote in. She asked for a children's page, a small comic and a corner for pen pals to be included in the paper. But top of her list came the request: "Tell the people more about the Wilson Rowntree boycott and tell them what not to eat that's Wilson's."

In another instance, a local doctor used the paper's columns to appeal for information from workers suffering from high blood pressure. Then there was the trade unionist who sent in advice, based on his factory's experience, on how to set up a workers' committee.

As *Grassroots'* implantation in the community has deepened, so has its understanding of its own role in the promotion of mass work. The result is a stronger-than-ever emphasis in linking trade union and community organizations with plenty of space given to activists to share views. Underlying everything is a simple argument. Struggling workers need the community organizations to assist in spreading word of their demands, in collecting money, in boycotting (where appropriate) companies' products and in convincing people that they shouldn't step into strikers' jobs. The community needs the local trade unions' help in fighting the kind of rent and bus fare increases which would otherwise swallow up any higher wages brought home.

Earlier attention given to "victory" type stories has shifted towards examining problems experienced and mistakes made by groups in factories and localities. More is being written, as well, about the traditions of the people's movement in South Africa. "Let's write the people's history" said a recent article suggesting that readers should interview elderly members of their families and neighbourhoods and send in their research to the paper.

On the organizational front future plans include special meetings in areas where the paper's circulation is still very patchy, producing pamphlets based on advice and information pieces which have appeared in the paper, publishing a manual on "How to produce community newsletters" and expanding on help given, locally and nationally, to groups developing their own alternative publications.

In South Africa today, since the Steyn Commission recommended a drastic tightening of state control over the established media in early 1982, journalists and editors have been intimidated into more self-censorship. And if the recommendations are implemented their effect could be devastating. This makes the importance of the community newsletter as an "alternative" medium greater than it has ever been. Yet the bigger the opportunities for newsletters, the bigger the potential dangers for them. Said *Grassroots'* chairperson at the last annual general meeting: "We can expect greater onslaughts to be made against *Grassroots*. We can expect greater demands to be made on it."

So when *Grassroots* concertedly canvasses community involvement, tries to decentralize its operation and share communication skills, it is doing far more than promoting participation. It is ensuring that, whatever happens, the democratic people's organizations linked to the paper will be able to go on educating themselves, sharing information and publicizing campaigns to draw mass support.

And these organizations themselves are certainly clear about where they are going. As one local CAHAC representative told *Grassroots:* "Our local rent, electricity and factory floor struggles must not be an end in themselves. We must link our local problems with the oppression and exploitation of our people in this country and the struggle for change."

MANUSHI
for women who speak out

# Woman power in print

The gift of 1,000 rupees* sent to the Indian feminist magazine *Manushi* by a reader was both a loving tribute and a political statement. "I am sending you this donation", wrote Usha Desai of Bombay, "in fond memory of my mother who suffered because she was a woman in this male-dominated society." It was the third anniversary of her mother's death, she explained. This gentle, intelligent woman had been married off at the age of four, received no schooling and became "maimed by smallpox and multiple pregnancies". Perhaps other readers, when remembering their dead, would help womanhood by helping *Manushi*.

Usha Desai is just one of a new generation of women in India who are determined never to live the lives of oppression and dependency forced on their mothers. *Manushi*'s pages are filled with the stories of many more... housemaids in Pune and tribal women in Surat striking for a living wage... a Delhi group staging an exhibition on the evils of dowry... students in Patna defacing poster images which degrade women... village women in Maharashtra protesting against

---

* One US dollar = Rupees 9.75.

price increases and sexual violence... women's organizations in Bombay demonstrating against rape...

The same magazine is a feast of fiction, poetry, cartoons and drawings by women who have mostly never been in print before. "*Manushi*", as one reader put it, "covers an incredible range of women's experience." Published simultaneously in English and Hindi, *Manushi* ("Woman") cuts across traditional divisions of culture, caste and religion in this vast country and succeeds in knitting together the ideas and actions of women of many different ages and walks of life. Its aim: "to be an open forum for (India's) emerging women's movement".

If the Delhi women whose inspiration it was had stopped to weigh up all the odds against them they might never have embarked on the project. They were a small group with no formal experience in journalism and none of the necessary technical skills. They did not even have a regular place to meet. "For a year," they remember, "we literally carried the *Manushi* office on our shoulders. We used to carry several bags of material and a borrowed typewriter with us wherever we went so we could sit down in someone's house, a park or a café, and begin to work."

The overall situation in which they were organizing themselves was, and remains, daunting too. There is the wholesale injustice which allows the well-off in India, assisted by Prime Minister Indira Gandhi's repressive policies and anti-trade union laws, to continue to preside over mass poverty. Then there is the horrendous injustice women suffer as a sex.

Indian women have a proud record of struggle in various peasants and workers movements, not to mention the national fight for independence. But for most of them the promise of equality inscribed in the constitution following independence has never materialized. Poor working women remain the most cruelly exploited sector of the labour force, on the land, where 80 per cent of the population still lives, and in factories and workshops of the cities.

Systematic neglect of women shows itself in the infant mortality figures — up to 60 per cent higher for girl babies in some areas — and in the glaring literacy gap between women and men.

Richer and poorer women in alike in many parts of the country are trapped in patriarchal family structures, passed off from one man to another and denied any real economic or social existence of their own. The dowry system, though officially illegal, goes on spreading — even percolating down to communities where it never existed before. Lack of economic independence leaves women especially vulnerable to sexual abuse and violence inside and outside the family. There have been numerous cases where brides have been burned to death by in-laws for bringing insufficient dowry. In Delhi alone 394 cases of burnings "by design or accident" were reported to police in 1980-81. Rape by individual men, by police, and by landlords' henchmen as a weapon of intimidation is a widespread phenomenon.

Yet those who decided to set up *Manushi* knew of women's groups emerging in different cities, of campaigns by women in both urban and rural areas, some of which had been brutally repressed by the government. They also knew that the mass media couldn't be relied on to report all that was happening.

Protests are usually reported in newspapers as unconnected, disruptive incidents, without any real examination of the grievances behind them. Problems like prostitution and rape are sensationalized. Dowry murders are reported in lurid detail while the dowry system itself is rarely questioned. And the prevailing image fed to women of themselves as decorative items to display consumer goods, as butts of cheap humour or as happy housewives, is a big block to building their self-confidence and action. Says the *Manushi* group: "We felt it was important to create our own media to collect and disseminate this information in a systematic way. There was a need to form an information network so that we could not only derive encouragement and strength from each other's experience, but also extend support when necessary."

The idea of the magazine first crystallized among a nucleus of students and teachers at Delhi university who in 1977 had started their own women's group there. Gradually in the course of a year, by making new contacts and organizing discussion meetings they built up a broad-based group of 25 people committed to the magazine project. Then they circulated for discussion to friends, women's organizations and trade unions in different parts of the country the following draft statement of aims:

We hope that *Manushi* will
*provide* a medium for women to speak out boldly and fearlessly,
*help to raise* questions in our own minds about the oppression we suffer individually and in society at large,
*generate* a widespread debate about ways of bringing about change and *move towards* a shared understanding for a common struggle,
*bring* women's organizations and activists in touch with each other,
*reach* women everywhere who want to break out of their passivity and isolation,

*enquire* into and re-evaluate the historical experience of women the world over,

*counter* the systematic distortion of the life situation and image of women, and trivialization of women's issues carried on by the mass media,

*and help to develop* a widespread information gathering system about women in different regions, communities, castes, classes, religious groups, work groups.

Encouraged by the warm reception and further promises of assistance that greeted this proposal, the core group pressed ahead with fund-raising. Their target was six issues in English and six in Hindi per year with more later if possible. Since literacy in India is so low among women and since the vast majority of the population live below the poverty line, they recognized that only a very small percentage of people could be reached through the written word. But within these overall constraints they hoped that by publishing in two languages and by pegging the price at one rupee, half that of the average Indian women's magazines, they would succeed in reaching a wide audience.

*Manushi* was intended to finance itself from subscriptions, from sales to bookshops and libraries, from well-wishers' donations and from advertizing. However, no advertisements would be accepted which portrayed women in "oppressive or stereotyped roles". And no grants would be taken from any institution, Indian or foreign. The group explains: "We feel that *Manushi* should live and grow on the strength of those for whom it is a felt need." The funding policy helped readers to feel that they were actively participating in *Manushi*'s development. It also ensured the journal's autonomy and commitment to the budding women's movement.

"*Manushi*, a journal about women and society", made its debut in January 1979. Its format set the pattern for future editions — plus illustrated features, fiction, regulars, poems, interviews and reviews. Countless hours had been put in by those involved, writing and translating articles, and learning layout and production techniques from sympathetic journalist and artist friends. They had tried to lay the foundations of a support network beforehand. Nonetheless, their venture was a complete act of faith. The 12,000 rupees raised initially was all swallowed up in producing this first issue. Whether money would be forthcoming to publish a second one they had no idea.

They need not have worried. Soon the letters started coming in. "I am a housewife who has spent most of my life in the kitchen. I could send you reports of women's meetings and demonstrations in this locality..." "We will try to get together a team to translate *Manushi* into Tamil..." "*Manushi* will be of tremendous use to our women's study circle..." "I'll make sure these copies go as far as I can get them in Hyderabad..." "I am a Hindi teacher — I showed *Manushi* to many women..." "We are translating the poems into Kannada..." "Send us more copies in Hindi because *Manushi* should reach the poor women of our society..." "We will send *Manushi* to all (our) Pacific and Asian Women's Forum members..."

The first issue yielded many subscriptions and offers of help, including some from men who still lend a hand with the magazine's distribution. Since then a new issue has been produced, on average, once a quarter and *Manushi* is travelling widely inside and outside India on its own momentum. The print run has topped 10,000 copies, about 20 per cent of which go abroad, to support groups and/or feminist resource networks in eight countries. There is also a high "pass on" readership of several women per copy.

After a year and a half, the *Manushi* workers decided to put less time into chasing advertisements, many of which proved unsuitable anyway. Instead, with some success, they introduced subsidized and unsubsidized subscription rates, explaining to readers the reason why. Subscribers who decided they could afford it were asked to pay the full cost price of 26 rupees for six issues as a way of helping the magazine. The others were charged 14 rupees (English) and 11 rupees (Hindi).

This dual system enables the Hindi edition which reaches a relatively low income group and makes a loss, to survive on resources generated by the English version of *Manushi*. It has also put the whole operation on a more stable financial footing although there have still been times when, after an issue was published, no money remained to mail it until volunteers dug a deep into their own pockets.

After its nomadic start, the Delhi group has found a permanent office in the flat of one member who teaches at the university. Neighbours in her street in one of Delhi's less opulent colonies are now well accustomed to the regular procession of callers and foreign visitors coming and going from number 202.

With a whole wall of meticulously shelved material and no unused corner in sight, *Manushi*'s one room looks like the nerve centre it is. It doubles as a meeting place for women's discussion groups, a temporary shelter for women in distress, and an aid centre for women seeking legal, medical or other advice. Its most familiar and much-loved face is that of the landlady of the house. A woman who has never worked outside the home or been involved in any political activity before, she has become so committed to *Manushi* that she acts as caretaker, accountant, welcomes visitors and even nurses other helpers when they are sick.

To keep the office open daily and the mountain of routine jobs under control, three full-time paid workers have been brought in. However the bulk of the effort of putting the magazine together is still carried out by volunteers. Two volunteers put in more than the equivalent of a full week's work fitted around the teaching jobs which subsidize them. A pool of ten others regularly undertake artwork and translations, reporting and distribution. A few more drop in on a more casual basis to assist with whatever urgent tasks are on hand.

While legal formalities led to the journal being registered as a non-profit trust with a named editor, there has always been a group effort behind it. Individuals involved therefore prefer to remain "nameless" except when they write articles, arguing that as *Manushi* is the effort of so many it would be wrong to single out a few for attention.

The group explains that *Manushi* has tried to work collectively because a hierarchical structure "would not only have inhibited our own learning process but discouraged others from participating". As it is, any woman who supports *Manushi* and wishes to help is welcome, whether or not she calls herself a feminist. All spheres of work, including editing, are open to anyone who shows an interest in learning extra skills.

Many readers have developed into effective "correspondents" for *Manushi*. In response to early appeals (*"Manushi* can become a meaningful venture only if you consider it yours-ours"), they have sent in all kinds of sketches, photos, news clippings translated from regional languages and reports of women's actions in their localities. Women's groups are asked to send in more than the kind of press release they might send to a newspaper. Critical reports are requested, using the experience of women who shared the action and not just the organizers.

Articles are never simply accepted or rejected, says the group. Rather, they try to write to the person concerned suggesting changes where appropriate or, if a piece is not suitable, explaining why. Though a time-consuming process, it seems to produce some creative results nonetheless. Several articles in the "One of Many" series in which individual women tell their stories, began life as readers' letters.

For any new reader of *Manushi*, the magazine stands out on three counts. Its information is designed to assist and link up women who are educating and organizing themselves, with particular reference to poor working women. It consistently explodes media-reinforced myths about women's "inferiority". And it unites women across political, religious and geographical boundaries.

Information comes in all shapes and sizes. A section headed. "Reports" carries items sent in from different parts of the country — exposés and news of fight-backs by women's and workers' groups. A regular feature, "Our Rights and Wrongs", looks critically at what legal provisions exist for dealing with discrimination and how different women have fared in bringing their cases to court. A history spot named "Her story" unearths accounts of the women who pioneered the early women's rights and social reform movements in India.

Always prominent are interviews with rural and urban working women in which they describe their efforts to keep their families alive while holding down the worst jobs, and their efforts to organize themselves.

Even the harrowing stories sent in by individual women of their lives and marriages testify that women can break out of their isolation by acting together. And combative editorials underline that women's so-called "personal" problems are political. "Most of our relationships at home and at work are unequal, are relationships of domination and therefore are assertions of power — political relationships... As soon as we start collectively to bring about change we are engaged in political activity, political organization."

On the media awareness front, one way *Manushi* tries to demolish popular myths detrimental to women is through its witty reviews of big box office Hindi and English films. As the reviewers often point out, even the heroines of modern Indian films, though allowed the occasional burst of rebellion, soon see the error of their ways and return to their "natural" role of self-denying wives and mothers.

Other *Manushi* articles have analyzed how humour in the press — cartoons, diary pieces, etc. — is used to trivialize women and peddle prejudice. Especially hard-hitting was the group's critique of Indian women's magazines, "The Media Game".

Based on a year-long study of three major magazines, the article was reproduced by the ISIS international feminist network in Switzerland and picked up by women's groups around the world. It began by stressing the ideological role of the media in general.

"The dominant mass media are owned and controlled by big business houses, the government, or both. By thus controlling the sources of information, news and the forums of public debate, these power groups can decide which issues to highlight and which to underplay." These media owners played different games with different oppressed groups, selling them different self-views and manipulating their concerns. "Workers' struggles are projected as 'law and order' problems, collective action against injustice as 'mob violence and rioting'."

"And in this game," the article continued, "women are special targets." It was a lot easier for exploitative social structures to be kept intact if the female half of the population saw itself in a self-sacrificing back-up role and so did not make its own demands for better living and working conditions.

*Manushi* then dissected the three Indian women's magazines in detail maintaining that, by dressing up drudgery, holding up "models" of attractive, efficient, devoted wives and evading women's real problems, they were a highly damaging influence on women's self-view and aspirations.

Printing its own readers' poems and short stories that portray women as courageous and independence-seeking is another way in which *Manushi* tries to counter mass media images. One issue of the magazine gave an entertaining feminist twist to a collection of well-known fables. They redeemed "wicked" stepmothers, suggested princes weren't always "charming", and said "fair" damsels could take care of themselves.

In line with its "open platform" policy, *Manushui* carries reports from a range of trade union, political party and civil liberties organizations active on women's issues, as well as by women who would not use any political label for themselves. In the same way the magazine reflects the different religious backgrounds of its readers and the views of women totally opposed to religion of any kind. Religion as a subject is discussed only in so far as it helps or hinders women's efforts to understand and fight against their common problems.

"The Media Game" article, for example, argued that religion and education, like the mass media, had been used to teach women "that the existing state of affairs is the best and only one". Another item reported a rural women's training camp where a Bible study course "dealt with the importance of women in Christ's vision of the world". One "Her story" feature examined how women had influenced and experienced the rise of Buddhism.

*Manushi* also encourages Indian women to see themselves as part of the growing women's movement nationally and internationally. Visiting activists from women's networks overseas are sometimes interviewed to compare thinking and experience on combatting problems such as rape. Material from foreign publications or feminist journals is reproduced: a piece on the conditions of Malaysian women factory workers... an open letter on disarmament from West German feminists to Soviet women... a report of the third international women and health conference held in Geneva in 1981... Suggested reading lists always include internationally-known authors. Letters pages always include some correspondence from overseas, often with news of *Manushi* support groups.

Not surprisingly, one such group has sprung up in the UK where isolation and racism confront many Asian women who have emigrated from India, Pakistan, Bangladesh and East Africa. The UK support group sells some 500 copies of each issue of *Manushi* to Asian women's organizations, bookshops, libraries and women's centres. Teachers and Asian community workers have used articles as resource material. Said a member of an Asian women's group launching its own magazine: "Reading *Manushi* made us realize the need for something for Asian women here." The reaction of Asian girls in a London youth group who read it was: "Aren't women strong!" And they loved the film reviews.

Feedback from inside India indicates that *Manushi* is acting as a catalyst for the emergence of new groups. The Delhi team often put women who help to distribute the journal in touch with other active women in their areas. This kind of contact has given birth to a number of study/action groups. Some are producing their own small newsletters and have been instrumental in getting *Manushi* articles translated and reproduced by other publications in their regions.

Some articles in particular have travelled far. The editorial from the first issue reappeared in half a dozen regional languages as well as in Sinhalese. An article on sexist advertisements entitled "Don't sell our bodies to sell your products" was translated into Punjabi in a regional newspaper *Jaikara*.

Social workers and rural development workers have used *Manushi* articles in literacy classes and discussion meetings and have invited women from the collective to speak at their conferences. One women's group in rural Madhya Pradesh started a community education programme in their villages using *Manushi* as educational material for the workers they train. This same group also paid the magazine an unexpected compliment by naming their new centre "Manushi Kendra".

Of the many campaigns in which *Manushi* has been directly or indirectly involved, one of the most important is a current effort to challenge the denial of land rights to tribal women in Bihar. Jointly with the All India People's Union for Civil Liberties, *Manushi* sponsored a committee of enquiry, sent to visit some 20 villages in the Singhbum district of Bihar. It found that in this land-hungry area, tribal women were being cheated out of their rights to inherit family land by a distortion of tribal law or were being forceably driven from it into destitution.

The committee submitted its findings in the form of a petition to the Supreme Court of India asking for the court's intervention. It also published the petition and its investigations in *Manushi*. Before these appeared in print, one local tribal movement had already translated the petition into Hindi, distributing it widely in booklet form. The battle is no longer simply a legal case but a growing broad-based campaign drawing in active individuals, women and men, and a range of political groups.

As the ripple effect of *Manushi* has grown, so its immediate circle of helpers has increased ten-fold, and this despite some serious setbacks at various stages.

Several women withdrew early on after tensions arose between some members of political parties who joined in and others who saw them as trying to "convert" the magazine. "We took a decision that while *Manushi* would always be an open forum for anyone to express their opinions, we would not like it to become a mouthpiece for any one political party/parties."

Another obstacle stemmed from the very problems the magazine was set up to counter. Many younger women who wanted to be involved encountered hostility from their families who prevented them from coming to the office. Unemployed, married women with children often couldn't find the time for consistent work at *Manushi* because they were so overburdened and tied down at home.

For the women most actively involved in *Manushi* it has been hard to achieve a collective way of day-to-day working since not all the people who turned up to help were able or prepared to put in the same amount of time and effort. Discouraged by this at first, the core group now takes a positive longer-term view. "Slowly we began to realize that different people are bound to walk at different paces and have to be left to decide how many steps they want to take at a time. To push them could be counter-productive. Also this struggle is bound to mean many different things to different women."

The core group feel very positive as well because, while they still carry the responsibility for getting the magazine out and the decision-making that goes with it, their immediate support group has mushroomed. Compared with 25 women at the start, 250 now help, the majority of them selling and distributing the magazine. Some 75 of these also join in discussions and meetings held under the *Manushi* umbrella.

So the evolution of *Manushi* has been exciting — and difficult. Extended intervals between one issue and the next testify to the continuing shortage of resources. The battle to involve more people in the magazine's central work and decision-making has still to be won.

However, *Manushi* today is better organized and enjoys broader overall support than its founders ever dreamed of. Few journals can claim to have staked their survival on the need and commitment of their readers to the point this one has, nor to have seen that faith so well vindicated. Its circulation may be tiny, especially if measured in terms of a country with a population as huge as India's. If measured in ultimate outreach and impact on women's lives, it is extraordinary.

# To sum up...

None of the groups featured in these stories even know of each other's existence. They are geographically scattered, born of very different situations. Half are working in the name of the church. Half are simply working in their own names and those of the people they try to serve.

In size they range from a staff of 200 and a five-million-dollar budget in the case of IPS, to a handful of people turning out *Manushi* from a New Delhi flat. Their tools of the trade are as complicated as satellite-linked teleprinters, as simple as drama props made from banana leaves.

Yet all these stories began in response to the same problem. Many people in their societies, these groups felt, had no voice — no adequate way of making their needs and concerns known. They had no voice because they lacked any significant access to, or control of, the means of communication to hand. It is a problem expressed here by people living in both wealthier and poorer countries, in free market societies where the media are mostly commercially owned and by those in countries where the state controls or where governments actively repress the media. On a world level it is expressed by the efforts of IPS to help the poorer nations find a voice in the international information order.

This common starting point has led, despite the surface differences, to many common experiences and conclusions. The groups' attempts to cut across existing communications structures have brought them under massive political or financial pressure, usually both.

Financially, the majority are far from self-supporting. Lacking the capital resources to withstand the economic recession, situated in poorer communities or countries and sometimes with the added handicap of raising money under the eye of repressive regimes, most rely on the church or outside agencies to make up their deficits. Even then their work is continually hampered by money worries.

Politically speaking, it is indicative that during the time this book was being written, two issues of *Grassroots* were banned, IPS was made the target of a damaging campaign, a correspondent for one of the radios was arrested and tortured, and two groups received "courtesy calls" from the police.

The groups which have tried to use existing communications structures for "alternative" ends have come up against additional constraints. Knoxville's Channel 20 has made it this far *despite* the prevailing market forces, not *because* of them. The team there ultimately has no control over how long it will be able to keep its little local access space. Similarly IPS, following the standard news agency practice of selling its material through intermediaries, has no control over how this material is finally used. Also because the agency is a sizeable venture competing in the world media market place it comes under continual pressures to fall in with the mainstream.

The stories from the US and Italy show that the development of communications technology which is technically and financially within reach of smaller groups or communities is no guarantee in itself of greater plurality. Cable television and Italy's free radio station began life as promising local media offering ample access for all. Within a matter of a few years they are being swallowed up by giant corporations as their wider profit potential is realized. In both countries the overall result is a very narrow selection of programmes for the number of radio stations or cable channels available and a reconquering for commercial purposes of spaces won by the community.

These stories show that those who contest the structures and use of the media rapidly come up against the power structures of society as a whole. Not only that, but the further they progress in trying to do what the existing communications channels are *not* doing, the more they have been confronted with just how much the media *are* doing to persuade the public, as *Manushi* puts it, "that the existing state of affairs is the best and only one".

From their direct experience as women, the *Manushi* group have analyzed how communication can serve to keep power and wealth fixed where it is by stereotyping and subtly undermining those who would demand a just share of resources and freedom from oppression. With the other groups this kind of critique is more implicit than explicit. All, however, have decided that they must address the communications problem as part of the much bigger fight for a better society even if, with the limitations inherent in their situations, they can only help to prepare the ground for that fight to an extremely limited extent.

For PETA it was a gradual realization: "We were confronted with nagging questions of what use these so-called artistic and technical tools were if they could not be used in alleviating... more pressing problems."

So these communications ventures are never seen as "neutral" professional inputs and never as ends in themselves. They are efforts to serve the community through communication while influencing in a small way the very context in which communication takes place.

This influence works on many different levels, often simultaneously. Consciousness-raising and the provision of basic information that people need to tackle immediate problems and take more control over their own lives creates the preconditions for change. Demolishing myths that undermine their confidence and unity is part of the same process.

But beyond this, most of the groups described here try to strengthen organizations and movements leading struggles around issues of land, labour, racial and sexual oppression. They give them a public forum, help them to discover their own history, to evelute their successes and failures and, most important, to link their struggles.

As CEDI says: "It's a movement when you put different kinds of fighters in touch with each other." In Italy the mass movement came first and created its own voice through the socialist radios.

Being linked up with a broad movement is also a source of support and protection for the communications groups themselves. Because, by definition, the biggest of them, IPS, does not have this, it is probably the most vulnerable. *Grassroots* on the other hand, operating on a smaller scale and in the harshest political conditions, confidently predicts that the community network it belongs to will always find a way to keep its work alive.

The participation of Protestant groups in Italian free radio is precarious. Radio Popolare, meanwhile, having consolidated its own broad constituency closely connected in turn with the labour movement and with its own system of paying supporters, is on a very different footing.

*Mecklenburgische Kirchenzeitung* could easily find itself out on a limb if it were not helping to build, and become an integral part of, a broad base of Christians who want to witness as critical supporters from within GDR society, not from the sidelines.

The groups' view of themselves as part of a wider effort to promote change and justice determines their whole style of operation. Some go to remarkable lengths to ensure democratic decision-making internally and active participation by those they are trying to serve. It is not just a notion that this is somehow A Good Thing. It has been time-consuming, unwieldy business, full of conflict. It has brought their work almost to a standstill at times. But it is seen as crucial by the groups who believe that their own organizations must reflect the kind of society they want to build.

One measure of the groups' commitment to participation is their openness to involving and training technically inexperienced people, some of them with hardly any formal education at all. Another is the value placed on the contribution of disabled people, women, and minorities whose insights and abilities are sharpened by oppression.

There is a continual tension between participation and professionalism. All the groups are convinced that professional skills are essential to reach a wide audience. They also believe professionalism can never be the only criterion. Thus through innovations such as volunteer-correspondents, readers' groups, training workshops and programmes edited and re-broadcast to build in audience opinion, they are taking some tentative steps towards involving the wider community.

Sometimes, they discover that the least educated and least confident people tell the most powerful stories, given help and encouragement. Sometimes, too, they themselves have had to "unlearn" the conventional communications values they had absorbed through previous training before they could be of real service to those around them. They have also learned that having once involved people you cannot impose priorities on them or force the pace. *Manushi* concluded: "Different people are bound to walk at different paces and have to be left to decide how many steps they want to take at a time."

It is because of their commitment that all these projects are in effect sustained by volunteers aided by paid staff, rather than the other way round. (IPS, situated in the very different setting of news agency structures, is the only exception.) For the same reason, all have an impact which cannot be measured by audience figures alone.

*Grassroots* has started a chain reaction in "alternative" media in the Cape and across South Africa. Like CEDI, *Manushi* and *MKZ,* its material travels far and has been adapted and reproduced for a wide range of information and educational uses. In fact, by strengthening local organizations to a point where their members are too busy to give as much time to the paper, it has almost put itself out of a job!

PETA volunteers, training people to train others, often never see the full fruits of their labours. But that fruits there are is evidenced by the growing network of educator-dramatists in South East Asia who look to them for a lead.

IPS is the David among the Goliaths of the press agency world, yet by its very example has caused more than a few rumblings in the Western media establishment.

Likewise, Radio Popolare, operating in the industrial heartland of Western Europe, offers a full-blown example of what communication with clearly declared social goals might look like.

Sometimes, without even setting out consciously to do it, these communications ventures have forged unity between people of many different beliefs and walks of life, in the case of *MKZ* between Christians and Communists, between Muslims and Christians, blacks and "coloureds" in the case of *Grassroots,* between women of different castes, peasants and city-dwellers in the case of *Manushi...*

Readers seeking communications possibilities which speak to gospel values will, I hope, find them in all these stories.

It is striking that those involved who are Christians and who are trying to practise a communications ministry, regard the "promotion" of the church as almost incidental to what they do.

Radio Enriquillo could have opted to become a religious station and made itself far more politically and financially secure. St John's, Knoxville, could have chosen to run its cable TV channel as an outlet for mainly religious programming, thereby gathering congratulations and probably boosting the size of its congregation. As members of struggling minorities in their countries, CEDI's Protestant founders, *MKZ,* and the Italian Protestant groups using local radio could have concentrated on raising their own public profile like many around them have done.

None of them ask for what CEDI referred to as "a Christian identity card" from those who join in their efforts. In the case of Channel 20 and Radio Enriquillo they deliberately keep religious programmes to a set proportion of the total output.

Radio Enriquillo, CEDI and *MKZ* depend on the church for moral and political back-up. Yet they are supported warily and regarded as dissidents in some church leadership circles because they are challenging sectors of the church as well as sectors of the society. They are trying to be as *MKZ* puts it "independent, not separate" from the church. It is no easy path to follow.

For me the Christians active in these stories witness by what they do, not by who they say they are. This is the basis on which groups like PETA, *Grassroots* and *Manushi* welcome Christians as partners in action. And it is certainly how those they set out to serve measure them. In my months of meeting so many committed and courageous people, I heard no greater tribute than that paid by a leader of the Haitian cane cutters to Radio Enriquillo. "Before the radio came" he said, "we were in the dark... Since we have found our voice through the radio we've become stronger and we will never go back to what we were."

a commentary by Martin E. Marty

# Righteousness and grace

This book presents stories of the ways in which groups of people communicate. Some are groups of Christians. Asked to make a series of theological reflections to set the stories into context for Christian readers, I am tempted to say that in many ways they do not need theological reflection. In their own way they are examples of theology and they contain within themselves the first hints of reflection. It may be that they are harbingers of a way Christians will write or "do" theology in the future.

Not for a moment does this mean that we should abandon historic modes of reflection. The Western tradition in philosophy and law, the great heritages of the Greeks and Romans are part of the mental "furnished apartments" in which we live. They will not disappear because of rebellions against philosophy, and they will be exported from the West to the corners of the earth whether they are welcome or not. Such ideas and modes of reflection stand behind much of the logic of modern medicine, weaponry, and statecraft. Many of the ideas issuing from the tradition are ennobling and some are demeaning, but in either case they are part of Christian reflection.

The philosophical roots of reflection live on in most of the world's Christian theology, whether in the West or not. Theology in this sense may be defined as the interpretation of the life of a people in the light of a transcendent reference — in the present case, in the light of divine activity, of God. In much of Latin America or Africa, where Plato and Aristotle have not been directly at home, modern Western agents of interpretation have been. It is not hard to see traces of Hegel, Kant, Mills, or Marx in such Christian reflection, sometimes to the detriment and sometimes to the enhancement of faith.

While not eager to abandon the Grand Tradition, Christians do well not to neglect the gifts of story as theology. In our time students of hermeneutics, of interpretation, have made much of narrative and what it discloses. Even among humans at the times when they make minimal claims to transcendence of the mundane, story is disclosive. Young lovers tell each other their past in order to become acquainted, to build trust, to dispel and retain mystery at the same time. Courts of law base decisions on precedent and story. Institutions gain strength from reflecting on their past in the form of story. Theodor Adorno has reminded us how important story is in efforts to be humane: history is the story of suffering and to neglect history, story, is to despise suffering past.

When humans experience the sacred or the transcendent, story is a characteristic way of interpreting. It has become almost a truism, a cliche, to note that story substitutes for or anticipates philosophical reflection in ancient Hebraic and modern Jewish transactions with the deity. The Hebrew scriptures have little to say about "being", "essence" or "substance". They have much to say about stories of beginning, of floods and sacred mountains, of burning bushes, exoduses, and exiles.

The stories which follow are not entirely unlike biblical parables, in which the mighty are or would be cast down, the first might become last, all is topsy-turvy.

These, second, are stories about media of communication, *mass* media we call them in the case of cinema, radio, television, or modern newspapers. Yet they reveal to us something about the nature of life today and about the media that would portray or shape common life. That is, there is not much of a common life or a common set of media. Of course, when a government has a monopoly on radio or television and broadcasts only its point of view, we may think of a truly mass audience. But that audience may be bored, sleeping, or ready to turn off the electronic instruments. Almost equally true, in societies where electronic media have commercial sponsors and there are few bands of communication, very large audiences may group. Still, with few exceptions — like the wedding in British royal family circles, or World Cup soccer matches — it is interesting to note how limited audiences are. Governments and commercial powers are constantly expressing frustration at their limits of "getting through".

This has meant that general circulation magazines have difficulty surviving, while journals for, say, left-handed yachtspeople or breeders of chinchillas prosper. Media have targets. Modern mass instruments have had to learn about sub-community where they cannot reach community. In this book communication takes advantage of mass devices to reach small yet sometimes decisive audiences. I wonder if many of the communications would interest people of a slightly higher or lower social class, a slightly more liberal or conservative theological cast, or whatever.

The theological reflector ponders, then, what this says about common humanity in the family of persons, about common life in the body of Christ. We are, more than we know, tribal and sometimes tribalist, though the tribes may be based on class or caste, denominations or aesthetic taste, and less on "blood". But that leaves the question: ought Christians aspire to employ media for the sake of seeking convergences, for developing larger community out of sub-communities? Should we surrender to the limits of specialization or imitate the powers of the world in making efforts to transcend tribe?

From these first two observations, about story as theology and stories of mass media as stories of sub-communities, a third reflection almost naturally grows. This has to do with the understanding of the purpose and focus of communications media in the hands of dedicated Christians. What is easy to overlook on first reading and most striking during a pause to reflect is this: without exception, these people choose to see or are forced to see communication as acts of purposiveness which belong, shall we say it, to the grim "work" portions of life.

Such a focus is understandable. Life is short, mean, brutish, grim, lived in the shadow of oppression, under the cloud of want, and in the prospect of death. No one seeks journalistic or electronic media in the hands of Christians or any one else who see life as nothing but entertainment, who inspire forced smiles of joy or dancing on graves. These may not be times of frivolity. But if there is ever a light touch, an ironic note, a tinge of humour, a grace note, a divine roar in the face of the oppressor, it does not come through in these reports. Even the theatrical groups have a kind of guerrilla grimness to them; so, at least, one gathers.

If my observation has any accuracy and merit, it may point directions for Christian communicators or those who seek stories to tell about them. For the highly purposive and productive "Protestant ethic" use of media displayed in some of these stories, one that is short on grace or *eros,* denies something about the nature of media and of the gospel.

A psychologist, William Stephenson, has written on "the play theory of mass communication". He notes that to publics, the use of media belongs ordinarily to play time, not to work time. People want to enjoy an evening at the cinema or theatre; they seek diversions through radio or television; even though the morning papers bring bad news, they list newspaper-reading time as a leisure activity. Communicators, television critics, publishers of newsletters or newspapers, then, have a distorted or unrepresentative view of media because for them communicating is work. One of the reasons for our small audiences may be that we so seldom are interesting and lively. We have important messages to transmit and they will be picked up by the already converted who need their information. But we do not readily engage new people. (That some of this book's stories succeed in such engagement is a cause for celebration.) Not all media need address the "play" dimension of life, but they might at least now and then in the Christian orbit inspire new ideas and loyalties and not merely reinforce existing ones.

That observation leads to the corollary in the understanding of the gospel. If I have appealed to William Stephenson's social scientific theories for the former, I would turn to the work of experts on leisure for the second: Josef Pieper, Hugo Rahner, or Walter Ong for example. Father Ong, in a foreword to a book by Hugo Rahner, points out that in the modern world the quest for freedom — which is what the gospel and most of the presently-discussed media are about — is often unfortunately and sometimes necessarily seen as dour, sombre, grim. Ong contends that such a monopoly in respect to outlooks on freedom is itself a partial surrender to the grim foe, the oppressor. In both biblical and Greek thought, the gods played, the God of Israel creates Leviathan for the sport of it, the biblical stories show people being tricksters, deceiving those who would keep them under iron hands, or finding grace to out-think, out-smart, out-believe, and out-last the enemy. We look for more of this in Christian communication.

Now, the rather sober and "righteous" expression that comes across in these stories results from another perception that has theological assumptions and overtones. In most cases, these are stories of communication in the face of great odds because they witness and act in the face of the oppressor. It may be that the story-teller has sifted them all through one grid or chosen one language of communication for the telling. But it is more likely that, as a faithful and accurate reporter, she is mirroring the assumptions and inten-tions of the people about whom she writes.

In all these cases, there is an almost Manichaean distinction be-tween gospel and non-gospel, oppressed and oppressor, good people and bad people, persecuted and privileged. I say "almost", because as one examines their workings it is clear that they are undertaken in the midst of ambiguity and self-criticism. Yet the presence of such patent foes inspires such natural frustration or fury that there seems little time for another element looked for by Christians: repentance, a sense of one's own finitude, sin, ignorance, limits, and self-interest.

Jacques Ellul speaks to this issue of repentance in a different con-text. As an author, he has not always been friendly to movements designed to throw off oppression. In his book on violence he has pointed out that sometimes freedom fighters are as interested in over-throwing the powers that oppose them as they are in actual represen-tation of oppressed people. Thus during the Vietnamese War, the proper denunciation of American foreign policy by dissident Americans sometimes seemed to him to be based as much on the desire to find one's own movement or party displacing the ad-ministration of Lyndon B. Johnson, "the oppressor", as on regard for the suffering Vietnamese. Who, asked Ellul, cares for the Sudanese, the unfashionable poor, those who, when represented, do nothing to change the internal politics of one's own land.

Critics of what I have just written are likely to dismiss it as the in-effective comment of a historian. Historians are always seeing com-plexity, ambiguity, reasons for ambivalence. They cannot act for these reasons, and must yield the field to almost fanatic and obsessed single-minded people made pure because they will one thing: revolu-tion, overthrowing the oppressor. Or they may say that I write from the luxury of academic tenure in the American upper middle class, a putatively secure position, one that does not breed empathy for the suffering of the world.

I must risk such anticipated criticism for several reasons. First, I yield to those who point out that there would be no revolution if history were in the hands of historians. Historians point out to the ways in which the formerly oppressed turn oppressor after the revolution, the ways in which we can see in retrospect that those who would eliminate violence breed new violence, those who would diminish suffering may — at least for the short pull — add to it. No, history cannot be only in the hands of those so caught up in the need to see one's own movement subject to judgment that he or she cannot participate in understanding *krisis* and acting in the name of an avenging Lord towards the birth of a New Creation.

Second, if one believes in a communion of saints and a variety of gifts, it is well that some tell stories of communicators who act in a spirit of righteousness with little evidence of self-examination and that others set those stories in the context of human self-deception, even when the humans may be virtuosos of faith, heroes and heroines, saints and martyrs. And we may add a third point, as an aside: it is well to foresee criticisms by enemies of all these ventures, Christians who readily side with oppressors or against those who would upset them. Let them know that we who issue this book have introduced a note of self-criticism along with the criticism of others.

On the positive side, if we remember that this book may be read as much in Western Europe and North America as elsewhere, we shall find reason to see a need for balance. The "hermeneutics of the poor", the need to read biblical and traditional texts within the reality of the hungry stomach, through the eyes of the poverty-stricken, is an element in this set of stories. All day, all night, one is bombarded by signals emitted from other sides, by those who have no reason to keep these realities in mind. In America there is an "Equal Time" doctrine, one that is to assure at least some measure of compensation for voices suppressed by power situations. This book is a part of Christian "Equal Time" venturing in a world where almost all other signals reinforce the status quo, the powers that be.

If one could penetrate beyond these stories and reach the editors, playwrights, cinematographers, and broadcasters whose stories these are, there would be reason to urge Christians into a deeper study of the Bible. Now and then on these pages biblical assumptions are implied, though when one reads that the church should represent "the Bible's" position, there is room for a question mark: *the* Bible's position? The Bible is a library written through ages, reflecting many situations and viewpoints. Much that it says about holy war is in conflict with Isaianic, Messianic, or Jesus-based words of peace, and their words of peace are uttered in the face of legitimations of war. What is *the* Bible's view? The Bible speaks consistently for justice, for siding with the poor, but offers little that is unambiguous about policy and strategy for fulfilling the mandates. Romans 13 provides theological justification for the state and Revelation 13 envisions its undercutting and overthrow. This book tells about the people who live under Revelation 13 more than about their struggles with their own understandings of Romans 13. Could it be that engagement across the lines of class, caste, and power in the face of biblical text will be for Christians a base for understanding each other's hermeneutics and giving expression to life in the body of Christ?

The Bible points out that not many wise, not many mighty were called, that God chose the weak to confound the wise. When one sees the minuscule budgets of these communicators, the tiny audiences, the barely measured effects, it is clear that faith in such a calling persists. Annual budgets of most of these ventures would buy fifteen seconds of commercial time in the American football broadcast season and cycle. Yet a God who speaks through poverty, weakness, and incarnation among the poor, may well be using these instruments to shape profound response, while privileged media reinforce superficial if still plaguing holds on the mentality of oppressors. One cannot read these stories without being moved by the examples of faith, dedication, and stewardship.

These communicators seem to have an intrinsic sense of the value of what they are doing. They have to be concerned about effects, for one does not communicate unless there is the communicated-to to help shape, through *praxis,* the communicator. Yet unflinchingly and unflaggingly, these communicators persist whether funds are plentiful or not — and they never are — or whether their sides are winning or not: they always are, but not as the world counts winning (2 Corinthians 5:17).

One may ask many questions of these stories: about the readiness of Christians to see their worlds through eyes of class-consciousness as much as through eyes of the New Creation of all in Christ; about the impulse towards instant politicization; about the neglect of many grand Christian themes. Still, it is fair to assume that in the repository of options that belongs to the Christian communion, with its marvellous diversity, there are other communicators who will voice or display catholic intentions, to manifest the marvellous and bewildering variety of a church that is both prophetic and compromised. The stories of that internal pluralism await another day, another telling, another book. For now, let there be marvels at the working of the Spirit through these targeting groups who move us by their zeal, their passion, and their skill at bringing forth more than expected from resources far too small.